A GAME OF SAILORS

Ken Evans

authorHOUSE®

AuthorHouse™ UK
1663 Liberty Drive
Bloomington, IN 47403 USA
www.authorhouse.co.uk
Phone: 0800.197.4150

Published by AuthorHouse   05/06/2016

ISBN: 978-1-5246-3275-5 (sc)
ISBN: 978-1-5246-3274-8 (e)

This is a work of Fiction. Names, characters, places, and
incidents are a product of the author's imagination. Locations
and public names are sometimes used for atmospheric
purposes. Any resemblance to actual people, living or dead,
or to institutions or locales is completely coincidental.

Print information available on the last page.

This book is printed on acid-free paper.

Contents

All the nice girls love a sailor
All the nice girls love a Tar.
Oh, there's something about a sailor,
Well, you know what sailors are!

FOREWORD

After all these years, and looking back, I could still see in my minds eye the river below reflecting the pale moonlight and the sweeping beams of yellow light from the searchlights, and the sudden spurts of orange tracers from the guns below, illuminating the cockpit with sulphur-coloured light and the other Heinkels holding their agreed formation, lumbering with their heavy loads, and the bomb-aimer lying stretched out in the front cockpit, following and counting in my mind the meandering bends in the river, waiting for the Millwall loop to come into view, and instructing the pilot to adjust the line of attack north to cover the target area.

And over all the years of my boyhood I would fly this mission many times, mainly as I drifted into sleep. Or sometimes to be awakened shockingly by the noise of the shrill air-raid siren shattering the quiet darkness of the night; the terrifying wail etched into my memory of all the other air raids I have known in boy-hood days, and my minds-eyes would automatically look down from instrument panel, even in my slumber, from the imagined cockpit, at the illuminated meandering serpent below glistening in the London moonlight.

And with much time, long after the war, there were other missions and expeditions and events that entered my memory by some strange alchemy to occupy my mind, and these memories also waiting randomly to carry me away, unlike books which knew their place and were always within easy reach and always at hand. But these memories of the sounds of war had burrowed deep into my soul, waiting over the years to intrude at the drop of a hat without as much of a `by your leave `.

But the river had always been there in one way or another, at or beneath my feet, from my earliest boyhood this muddy disorganised place, invented by the gods, my boyhood playground and a place of escape from my pleasant but claustrophobic home-life; but too often the thoughts of the river kidnapped me, swallowing me whole, to be re-born as anything other than a thin small boy!

Was it this, my primary experience of my relationship with flowing water a river that determined the flow of these thoughts, my embryonic world-view, my ontology, …my way of being ? Or was it more like the making of a mosaic of memories of tiny events slotted together over time, which hinted at some tolerably coherent picture that might be me?

Yes might be me ? For that was the essential question that followed me all the days of my life; even here there is a resonance, as there is in every single utterance, every single word, every single thought; most of which are beyond recapture.

I should be able to make sense of this; as simple as threading a needle perhaps, but whenever I begin to see it clearly so to jot down the simplest points, other fragments of shadows of remembrances vie for attention.

Obviously it is more than influences of time and place that make a person, important as these must be as context and background, and also more than formation of habits created through the minute incremental and repetitive daily activities such as teatime which shape a life, each with its profusion of shared and personal meanings. But there is more to any man than this; but at least it's a start!

SKYRAIDER

1950 August,
Fulwell Road, Teddington.

Skyraider, the magic wasn't just in the name; but in her big-girl style and her slightly comical Rumpity-like appearance, and of course her responsiveness to our sometimes unfair demands. And I guess it was almost the same with Jean M, the frisky young daughter of one of my mother's friends who arrived at our house one sunny afternoon sometime, late-Summer 1950.

On that occasion both her mother and mine suggested that we should go to the park for a walk whilst they chatted. It was a hot and sweaty day and we walked and talked and eventually we sat down by a small pool to cool off, and eventually the girl, Jean asked me if I knew how to kiss; I admitted that I had never tried it, and she immediately instructed me to close my eyes and she would show me how.

She held my head with both hands as if it were somehow completely detached from my body and turned it to face hers, and I closed my eyes; I could sense her warm breath on my face and the sweet smell of her skin as her lips touched mine and then quickly withdrew; I was stiff with fear! "Don't hold your mouth closed like that, and relax." She demanded. "Don't you know how they kiss in the films?" I was scared as she closed in again, her wet mouth on mine, and her tongue moving between my lips, forcing them apart. I hadn't expected that, but somehow she had unlocked my resistance. "Use your tongue!" She panted, and like two small snakes our tongues were wriggling in and out of each other's mouths. I was seventeen and something unbelievable had just happened, not unlike learning to fly, and going solo for the first time!

Tuesday 18th September 1956
Royal Naval Air Station Culdrose, Helston Cornwall.

After a week of Harry-Clamper's, the heavy fog-like grey sea-mist native to the Lizard began to clear, the late-morning sun breaking-through, beaming like a good omen, bathing the airfield in a dazzling radiant light, the sharp-bright light now glancing off the outlines of the Boss's aircraft fuselage and tail-plane, creating a ghostlike glare as I followed him in-line, taxiing along the perimeter towards the main runway ready for take off.

With very little cloud overhead and the remains of a dissolving frost on the dark-damp tarmac, and the usual few airfield hares chasing one other across the wet grass; but apart from this, the remainder of the airfield is eerily and silently deserted as our four dark-blue Cabs (aircraft); Skyraiders of 849 Squadron C Flight, chugged slowly into place at the end of the main runway. When maneuvering my Skyraider into place on the perimeter she has the appearance of a lumbering and clumsy-looking over-weight dark noisy contraption, but once airborne she is deceptively agile and a beautiful aircraft to fly.

I bring my Cab to the start of the runway and line-up alongside the 'Boss'; Lieutenant Commander 'Paddy' Sullivan, Commanding Officer of C Flight 849 Squadron, and look across to him to give him my thumbs-up, ready for take off. The remaining two aircraft join us, and take-up their position close behind as we await 'Clearance' for takeoff from Air Traffic Control. Looking around I see the other two pilots in their cockpits completing their final pre-take off checks; operating their flight-controls; moving ailerons,

3

tail-fin, throttle etc., and grab a quick last look round at the surrounding airfield seemingly still slumbering. In that stillness the only sound, our four noisy Sky Raiders, awaiting to depart Royal Naval Air Station, Culdrose located at the tip of the Lizard Peninsular, Cornwall; our destination HMS Albion, our 'Mother' ship, our Aircraft Carrier presently steaming somewhere off the northern tip of Spain.

Each of our four crews of pilot and two observers, had become experienced in our routine duties; AEW (airborne early –warning) surveillance sorties, which we flew singly and individually, but this morning is different and unusual. Not because there are four of us flying together; that is normal when we are returning to our Carrier, but on this occasion the unusual element was the surprisingly sudden termination of our main annual leave, and the unexplained hurried preparation for departure to our ship, and the visible sense of urgency as we waited to take-off.

The whole of C Flight had been informed only a week before, by telegram, for all aircrew to return to Royal Naval Air Station - Culdrose, our land-base, and the rest of the squadron personnel to report directly to Portsmouth; HMS Albion's Home Port. There had been no further information or explanation for this decision, but speculation had it that we were to prepare for 'an extended U.N. Fleet exercise somewhere in the Atlantic, and then perhaps onto the US for a showing-the-flag visit.

However word had come back from our ground-crews already aboard Albion at Portsmouth that the ship was taking-on large amounts of unusual supplies including heavy armament; with 20 mm ammunition, 500lb. and

1000 lb. bombs and air to ground missiles! Something was obviously afoot; but whilst on leave we were all too intent on living it upto consider any national news that might involve us, or our squadron.

I hear over the R/T the Boss reporting to the Tower all Pre-Flight Checks- Complete and the Tower clears us for Take-off; the Boss indicates 'a Go' with a hand-wave and opens his throttle; indicated by the billowing clouds of blue-grey exhaust smoke streaming from his engine and over his main-plane beneath his cockpit, as he lurches forward picking up speed along the runway. I wait watching his tail-wheel clear the ground about half-way along the runway before I release my own brakes and follow suite, opening -up my throttle to eighty percent and listening for the engine's deep throaty roar and settling into her steady rhythm, and then full-power. A quarter way along the runway, at about 140 knots I briefly nudge the control column forward, enough to feel a point at which the tail-wheel clears from the runway, and the main wheels stop bouncing, and immediately feel the ground slip gently away beneath me, like discarding a heavy overcoat.

My big-blue bird is back in her natural environment! There is nothing like that moment for any pilot when his Cab unsticks from terra-firma and the machine is entirely in his hands; he and his aircraft instantly becoming subject to an all-together different set of physical laws; not the ordinary laws that hold human-kind tied to terra-firma, but the laws of flight in their mystical formula; where thrust overcomes drag and lift overcomes gravity and man and machine becomes (so it seems) lighter than air, like a bird in flight!

Quickly, I search for Boss ahead, and an even quicker glancing check of my flying panel; everything as it should be, I raise wheels and flaps and ease the throttle back; as I come alongside Boss, airspeed now 220 knots, together in a gentle climb to five thousand feet where the others catch-up and the four of us move into a loose square formation, with about the space of six wingspans between each of us; I now level with Boss as his 'Number Two', or Wingman as the Americans would have it, as we cross the long line of pure-white foam that divides land from sea along the Cornish coast. A voice cuts-in from Culdrose Tower wishing us 'Bon Voyage', the Controller monotonously reading a weather forecast and giving us a provisional bearing which should take us to somewhere in the vicinity of the North-West coast of Spain. We all switch to C Flight's 'A'- channel on the R/T to check with each other; everything satisfactory; as we continue climbing to an altitude of eight thousand, leveling-off and trimming our cabs, reducing airspeed to cruise at about 180 knots and flying virtually hands-off; these lovely girls are designed to almost fly themselves!

Each of the four crews of 'C' Flight know this part of the English coast, eastward from the tip of Cornwall to the start of the English Channel; it being the start of our usual route when on (AEW) aircraft-early warning sorties, our almost daily routine practice when flying from Culdrose, and our main responsibility, and for which our Sky Raiders were specially adapted, with their huge bulbous bulging 'ray-dome' slung beneath the fuselage giving an appearance of a pregnant Guppy, but containing a large and powerful revolving radar scanner, giving us a radar range of a two-hundred miles diameter. Our primary object to search the skies for other military aircraft, which might pose possible threats to our national airspace.

With our equipment's Radar range of 200 miles, we could easily locate our Mother-Ship ourselves without any further assistance from ground- control or instructions from our Carrier. This radar equipment is operated by my two Observers cramped in a dark separate cockpit built into the fuselage just behind the mainplane (wing); claustrophobically dark and with the tiniest oval windows set into the two small access doors either side of the fuselage. So each Cab has a crew of three, and she belongs to us and we to her.

My Observer crew; both 'Suby's; Sub-Lieutenants ('Danny'Daniels and 'Paddy' Niblock) who joined the Squadron six months ago, and I, now in my eleventh month on the squadron, so technically we are all still 'Sprogs' together, and we get along as if we are part of a schoolboys sports team.

This is my first Squadron-posting after completion of Flight Training, although I had the option of moving onto Jets, but fell so much in love with Skyraiders towards the end of my flying training on Corsairs, also a prop - powered aircraft, that I opted for 849 Squadron, and her American Skyraiders; leased to us as part of an agreement between our government and the US, and which also included my 'instruments and night flight training' on this Cab, in Pensacola, Florida, (of all places!) so for a while I lived the life of an American 'Jockey', their term for a 'standard' military pilot, but which I have since come to appreciate is a fair description of what I actually do when flying long and sometimes tedious routine surveillance sorties, as a Cab-driver.

Some of the other jet squadron crews I know, flying Venoms and Sea Hawks, occasionally jibe us and our propeller-driven Cabs as the last of the dinosaurs, but for me this aircraft has character, she is big and 'blousy' and obviously American, and built like a tank or a 'shit-brick –house'- as the maintenance crews claim, with her deep-throated din of her powerful Wright-Cyclone eighteen cylinder engine, roaring like an giant version of my own little red MG; which I love much for much the same reason, for it's throaty-exhaust song.

We leave the tip of Cornwall and cross the coast due south of Porthleven; below us the usual Channel ferry-traffic and larger vessels are on their daily business routes, spreading out from English ports like insects on a pond; I wonder if they are even aware of our presence over-head? Our ship HMS Albion has already made contact, and reassured us of good weather flying conditions, she on a course due West steaming in the direction of the mid-Atlantic, well clear of any regular shipping lines, and making ready for our arrival.

We maintain our comfortable cruising speed in our loose square formation; with the sun on our faces we can relax slightly and take in the sheer pleasure of flying. At this height the pond looks like a sheet of hammered grey metal, no indication of winds or waves, but I know this could change almost in an instance.

The Skyraider's cockpit is Spartan and bare; with no frills or padding, flying controls all close at hand and easy to operate; the interior sides above the controls exposing the metal fuselage inside ribs painted in a dull green protective paint; I can count the lines of rivets and the areas where the paint has been rubbed away exposing shiny aluminum rivet-heads; some of that wear no doubt mine!

A few occasional adjustments to trim the aircraft from time to time; for one of the characteristics of this prop-driven machine, especially with such a powerful engine of two thousand seven hundred horses, is a tendency to drift to the left which we all need to adjust to maintain our agreed distance between Boss and myself; actually this is almost intuitive now, even after only a few flying-hours in a Skyraider, which permits the occasional irrelevant intrusive thoughts, (actually fragments of thoughts) such as trying to recall the face of the girl I met just two days before the end of my leave, and of our slightly sad farewell, and the several possible reasons for our rapid return to duty, and the need to check that my tail-wheel is unlocked before landing onboard!

Our R/T frequencies are changed daily so we should be secure against prying ears; Boss has spotted Albion and indicates with a downward pointing finger, announcing that we will make our descent to 800 feet for a fly-over salute and then to break-off to a nose to tail formation for our preparation for landing-on. Even from a thousand feet the Carrier Deck looks ridiculously small, one might even say impossibly so, by far, on which to land a Cab the size and weight of a Skyraider, but we have to manage it anyway! We tighten our formation for the Fly-over and I take-in the view as we approach; sea conditions relatively calm; I have seen far worse, but its almost impossible to calculate the various changing forces acting on a carrier steaming into wind with constantly changing tidal-currents contributing to sudden surges in speed, causing side to side *sway*, and the up and down heave of the ship, with each axis contributing to the *pitch*; *roll* and *yaw*, and besides this the possible changeable side-winds at that final critical moment of touch-down; but yes, we manage it somehow with technique and practice and a bit of luck!

Albion Air-Traffic Control clears us for recovery (landing-on) and we throttle back; Boss is now about a mile ahead and starting his first 90 degree turn to port, the left, and a further two 90 degree turns and is now flying up-wind at about 600 feet and beginning his final approach, his landing gear and flaps fully down, hook down and descending to about 350 feet. Around this point he should be able to access the ships Optical Landing System; a huge mirror with it's system of lights which produce a green line across the middle of the mirror indicating that an aircraft is on the correct 'glideslope'; the ideal is to keep the orange (meat) ball of light in between the two halves of the horizontal green line. If this is achieved the Cab should make a satisfactory landing and the arrestor hook catching one of four arrestor wires stretched across the flight deck within the first fifty feet of the aft-end of the deck. Besides this, as an added benefit there is the Talk-Down of the Flight-Deck Captain who is also an experienced pilot, and will help us to compensate for any of the final second's many 'fluctuations', which can interfere with a 'good-landing'.

The Boss caught the third wire, and executes a good three-point landing. I can see the deck handlers signaling him; 'Brakes-On' and to 'Raise Hook' and indicating taxiing forward, folding wings as he taxies to the starboard 'Parking Station' (Fly-One) forward of the ship's 'Island', and clearing the Deck for my landing.

I turn into wind, open the cockpit canopy and feel the fresh biting - cold wind on my face. Wheels and flaps down - check, adjusting trim to bring the nose up, changing the aircraft's attitude for a three-point landing. Hook down, and tail-wheel unlocked, although a locked tail wheel, which prevents it swiveling, is helpful for maintaining control of direction when landing on a land-based runway, the reverse is necessary when deck-landing because the uncontrolled 'pull' on the arrestor cables can skew the aircraft to one side or the other depending on the point the hook catches the wire, and a swiveling tail-wheel helps compensate for this.

The final 90 seconds are critical, everything happens so quickly, *in literally split-seconds,* in which to make corrections or to open up for a 'Bolter', to go round again. Landing a Skyraider on small Aircraft Carriers is not unlike coaxing a heavy-weight bird onto an undersized perch, and is more art than science; of sensing the constantly changing forces acting on the aircraft, and tweaking the controls to bring her onto a spot, fifty or so feet long to catch an arrester wire. With exactly sufficient throttle to maintain a steady descent, ideally slow enough to almost 'float' down without stalling, a touch of aileron to bring the orange ball back to the center of the mirror; and Johnny Eagleton's, the Flight-Deck Captain's familiar voice cuts-in, talking me down, "Slight-Left, …lose-height, …Correct *Glideslope*,…. OK!"

I feel the sudden harsh *reassuring* pull of the arrester wire jerking me back into my seat, and the squealing thud of my wheels on the deck; instantly throttling back,… I'm down! "Thanks Johnny!"

The Flight-Deck Aircraft-Handlers rush out of the cat-walks and unhook me and unravel the arrestor-cable, looking up at me and signaling instructions; 'hook-up and fold-wings', they need to clear the landing area quickly and guide me forward alongside the Boss's Cab forward of the ship's Island. I cut the engine, prop spluttering to a stop; my dark-blue beauty seems to heave a final sigh of relief. One of the maintenance crew is already up on the main-plane (wing) helping me to disentangle myself from my chute and dinghy straps, as if their umbilical connection has to be broken before I become fully land –based, or on-board, sea-based again. I wait with my two Crew-Men, who are now out of their cramped Cubby-Hole, watching while the other two Cabs are recovered, and we make our way below decks to the 'Briefing Room' to be welcomed aboard by the Ops-Officer. And then, one at a time assisted through the passageways and down ladders to our Cabins near the Wardroom. This time I get to share a Cabin with a 'window', in other words above the water line. It's surprising what a huge perk this is; to be able to see the sky and breath fresh sea-air as I awake from my bunk.

The Jet squadrons were already recovered on board; 800 and 802 Squadrons with 20 Seahawks between them, and 809 with 7 Sea Venoms; together a powerful strike-force if ever it's needed. That evening in the Wardroom there was plenty of speculation about the sudden cancellation of main leave, the general agreement was that it was part of an exercise in the Fleet's readiness for emergencies, but most of the conversations drifted back to local events and

Nights out on the Town, some in London's West End; with shows and Dinner-Dances around Mayfair, Piccadilly and Hammersmith Palaise.

Looking around at the new faces during Dinner in the Wardroom I thought I noticed an old school acquaintance; not really a pal but someone who lived in Teddington not far from my home, I couldn't remember his name, if I ever knew it, but he was the only *other* boy in my school's sixth form with red (ginger) -hair. When I approached him later it seems we must have enlisted about the same time; I thought it strange that we had not bumped into each other before; he was now an Observer, flying in Sea Venoms in 809 Squadron; he seemed very jumpy as if he wasn't too sure that he wanted to admit our acquaintance. But anyway it was a pleasant evening with even the ship's Chaplain drinking his share of shorts!

The following morning one of the Stewards informed me at breakfast that there is a muster of all aircrew in the Briefing Room at 0900 Hrs; I had assumed that there would be no flying for at least a day; as there were no further instructions on the Daily Briefing Board, so I took it that it was to be a general briefing about the expected forthcoming Exercise, when in fact it was about 'Target Practice' for the Jet Squadrons, and for 'C Flight' to fly early warning Combat Air Patrols around the ship, commencing at 1100 hrs., which means us donning 'goon-suits', a two-piece waterproof flying suit, very uncomfortable to wear but necessary when flying over large stretches of cold water, as ditching in the Atlantic could mean a quick death from hypothermia!

Our Skyraiders are strictly for air surveillance and that is our purpose, so we carry no armament, on the other hand the Sea Hawks and Sea Venoms are fighters capable of carrying rockets and bombs besides being equipped with 20 mm cannon, so their pilots need target practice; they are briefed in the main Briefing Room while the rest of us use the Aircrew Annex, which includes a small refreshments area, and which is usually used as a kind of Rest and Locker Room. The Boss briefs us on operations, and also informs us that the whole ship's company would be exercising for a higher state of the ships 'Readiness and Action Stations', which means that sometimes certain parts of the ship would be isolated by closing and locking waterproof hatches and doors, and that we would need to know where we need to be at all times, otherwise we could be either locked in or out! This was one of the 'difficulties' of being an 'Airy-Fairy' in the Royal Navy; we are neither fish nor fowl!

Although Fleet Air Arm Crews received the same basic RN Officer leadership training as the Navy proper (but much shorter), our focus is on operating our aircraft; we know almost nothing about running ships, and it is this difference between us and Executive Branch Officers which leads to us to being referred to as slightly dainty 'Airy-Fairies', with a slight hint of not quite being real sailors or 'real men', which in turn has led us to refer to them as 'Fish-Heads';(Fleet Air Arm ratings refer to them as 'Hairy-Arses'), but we are not so 'unmanly' not to know about closing waterproof doors during Action Stations as a requirement of Damage-Control. Everyone on board knows that if a part of the ship is damaged and some compartments flooded or on fire, that it can be closed-off to prevent further damage and prevent the possibility of the ship sinking!

The largest and most vulnerable internal space on an Aircraft Carrier is the Aircraft Hangar, used mainly for aircraft maintenance. All the doors from passageways and other compartments are kept watertight with locking handles at all times, and there are massive asbestos fire-curtains, which are capable of shutting – off areas in the event of fire. It would be self-evident to anyone walking around the ship that the large Hangar is the ship's most vulnerable space to the possibility of causing sinking in the event of flooding or fire. And in the event of an attack our air-capability makes us an obvious target to an enemy, hence we are protected from the sea by Frigates and Submarines and from the air by our Skyraiders, and the entire workings of ship's machinery and crew's purpose is to enable our aircraft to take off and land. By comparison we have the more 'manly' job because unless you have actually experienced landing a more than half a ton aircraft on a carrier flight-deck in a heaving sea with a gusting head-wind, and perhaps in half-light it would be impossible to imagine how scary it really is, but perhaps it is it's scariness that makes it so compelling!

There is very little time for day-dreaming, for thinking about other matters; about girl-friends or shore-leave and other things, not that I had any serious relationships; because once back into the ship's routine we are all rather like chess-pieces, more or less either on duty or sleeping. But there are moments when the odd thought or other feelings bubble-up from nowhere to distract me, and others.

ALBION

Albion is a twenty-four thousand tonnes grey metal container of machinery, aircraft, men and their provisions. Her lower-half shaped like a sleek warship, her upper half a seven hundred and forty foot long flat rectangle of floating airfield, and bearing no resemblance to her Royal Naval forbears of that name. All names of Naval ships are recycled and my Albion is the eighth to bear that proud name, with her crest of a Lion seated on a white rock surrounded by an azure sea, symbolizing England, the land of white cliffs, and dubbed Albion by the conquering Romans in 55BC; that name has a long proud history! And although this metal canister of many deck-levels, compartments, passages and gangways; in fact a huge and complicated three-dimensional labyrinth in which all initially get lost, becomes the heart and home to sixteen hundred men and which eventually itself becomes a living entity with the constant heart-beat of her vast 76, 000 horse-power engines; a constant twenty-four hourly reminder that she is alive and well, and therefore all are well who sail in her.

To those of the outside world who rarely see the sea but might have perhaps seen a photo of Albion, there is really not much to see from her exterior, but to those whose lives depend on her she is mother and 'sweetheart', providing every kind of nourishment and comfort, such as it is; for as a Royal Naval vessel she embodies the history and traditions of Nelson's Day, still following similar strict social-class divisions between officers and men! Some sailors still sleep in hammocks; with which they have a kind of umbilical relationship, for should they die at sea they will be sewn-up in these canvases and their bodies committed to the Deep, to sleep in 'Davie Jone's Locker'!

Ordinary sailors and non-commissioned officers, (POs and Chief POs) of whatever standing are referred to as Ratings, accommodated in their crowded Mess-Decks, all situated in the forward part of the ship, while Officer's quarters are traditionally Aft, the rear of the ship, and between these two separate social and administrative worlds there is the traditional barrier of a contingent of Royal Marines; in other words Soldiers who could be trusted to protect the Officers in the event of mutiny; a historical nicety!

To an ex-grammar schoolboy Commissioned through 'Direct Entry', and not even into the Navy proper (men who sail and drive the ships), but as an 'Airy-Fairy,' and not even through the preferred route of a Dartmouth Cadetship, I sometimes pick up hints of snobbery from other officers who came through the hard route, but that is part and parcel of being Fleet Air Arm aircrew; our world is in the present while much of which is purely Naval is tied to the past; we tolerate one another! Fortunately my quarters among the eight cabins along one passage-way is occupied solely by aircrew; we fly round-the-clock and we leave 'Don't Disturb' notices on our cabin doors when we sleep, which can be any time of night or day; we don't live by ship's time of 'three Watches', but by operational flying schedules, but we also have a few 'ship's duties' such as overseeing working groups, as Divisional Officers with pastoral responsibilities for small groups of ratings, or as Duty Officer of the Day, for odds and ends when tied up in port. But at sea we are either flying or trying to sleep.

The girl I had met a few days before my leave was cancelled is a friend of my sister and lives in Hammersmith; her father runs a posh London Hotel, the choice of visiting American film and recording stars, and was currently hosting Johnny Ray an American singer whose act includes crying real tears, and was in the Guests' Bar the evening of my first date with this girl. And so we ended up at her place, or should I say her father's place where Johnny Ray happened to be enjoying a private party, and I was sort of pulled in. I had never heard of him prior to this celebration but apparently he was all the rage among the record-buying public and especially of young women, and was in London, performing at the Palladium.

It wasn't so much a party as an opportunity for a clique of theatre people to have a get together, and it was also my chance to see Julia in her natural environment and to admire her casual elegance and amazing self-confidence, so-much-so that I almost forgot about my own presence there, and who I was; feeling like a child at a stranger's birthday party!

So when her father spoke to me and asked me what I did for a living he seemed to have been startled by my matter-of-fact reply, and perhaps my boyish appearance, as if he was trying to fit me into his own idea of a Naval pilot, and revising his impression of me. But he smiled in a friendly way and offered me a drink; which suggested that perhaps I met with his approval!

But two days later unexpectedly, I was back in the Hotel at another little impromptu farewell party; this time given for me, because Julia had told him that my leave had suddenly been cancelled by a telegram from the Admiralty; it all sounded so important the way she explained it to both her parents. Her father toasted me as if I were about to become a war hero, and now not quite a month since that farewell, I can hardly remember her face, but I could still sense her lean-boney Virginia Woolf-like elegance. I didn't even know her address so I couldn't write to her, but occasionally in my thoughts I drafted a few sweet words to her, where their sentiments softened the perpetual whirr and hum of the Carrier's constant noisy heart-beat.

After a full-days concentrated target practice for the jet squadrons three hundred miles west, off the Spanish coast, and steaming south we entered the Straits of Gibraltar and headed a further two hundred miles sailing up and down just off the coast of Morocco, where the ocean is no longer grey, but a deep blue-green in which the Albion Flight Deck, seen from the air, sparkled like a beautiful silver jewel. Flying south along the Moroccan coast in the early mornings so invigorating! The bright sun on my face and enjoying the simple pleasure of observing the massive swell of the sea breaking on the yellow strip of sand along the north coast of Africa, way beneath me, and further inland the scattered small towns and villages dotted along desert sands casting their elongated shadows.

And when necessary we combine our surveillance exercises with mail-runs; carrying bags of mail to and from the ship to any of the pre-arranged military air bases around the Mediterranean coast. It requires two Skyraiders flying without our Observer crews in the rear cockpit to pick up all the twenty, or so, large mailbags from The French Naval Air-Base at Marseille. And I certainly felt the extra load on the return flight, but found myself thinking about the good and bad news I might be delivering! We recovered (landed-on), mid-afternoon after the jet squadrons had finished their target practice for the day and had already been recovered on board. As I taxied forward to our parking area the Flight deck, wings folded, several aircraft handlers were welcoming us as benevolent Postmen and eager to unload their mailbags. Alas I knew there would be nothing for me, but by the time we had completed our debriefing and returned to our cabins the Tannoy was already announcing that mail was "Ready for Collection".

The Tannoy is the relentless voice of the ship; in fact there is no escaping it, there being nowhere in the ship where it's voice is unable to penetrate, except in special circumstances, for example in Wardroom passageways where Aircrew are sleeping before and after Night flying, when it is muted, but even then, not completely switched off. It carries the voice of the ships Bosun, who in previous times would have communicated with the ship's crews by Busun's Call (a painfully high-pitched whistle), which is so shrill on the ears, it is said, that it would awaken those from their final rest in Davy Jones' Locker, and which even in these modern times still precedes all important announcements.

For a few hours after 'Evening Rounds' the Tannoy becomes 'Radio Albion', which is piped to rating's Mess Decks (their living and sleeping quarters) and (Flats) other communal areas throughout the ship, playing 'Record Requests' and a skittish interview programme called 'Down Your Hatch', modeled along the lines of the BBC's own 'Down Your Way'. Radio Albion is run by would-be DJs along the lines of a 'Pirate' radio station but is interrupted from time to time for 'executive' announcements.

To get from one place on the ship to another it is necessary to move between decks and gangways and pass through Rating's mess-decks and their shared spaces; all of which are blasting out their 'Record Requests'; songs competing with the whirr of ventilation fans and the constant deep hum of the ships turbine engines and a cacophony of many other indefinable vibrations; this is the voice of 'Albion', which would be less memorable if unadulterated by its background noise!

But despite this and remarkably, fragments from Elvis's 'Hound Dog' and 'Blue Suede Shoes', and Bill Hayley's 'See You later Alligator', Fat's Domino's 'Blueberry Hill', etc., and songs from the films such as 'Carousel' still managed to wheedle their presumptuous way through the barrages of noise, and impose themselves on my memory; for I frequently and quite suddenly found myself humming a few lines or even a few words of songs I didn't even know I knew, or liked; and feeling further irritated at not being able to identify them! I suppose this must have been a small bit of unintended 'brainwashing' on the part of the DJs. And strangely, at times, I also began completing a kind of musical crossword in my head, linking phrases and words with other thoughts, and discovering that Rogers and Hammerstein's music especially, had resonances with real feelings, or perhaps those I hoped for or imagined?

At the very least they were food for thought in my crowded daily routine; flying sorties and fitting in with other 'ship's duties'.

The next four days were a mad panic to make the ship fully operational, in other words ready for war; which included the jet squadrons target practice, firing rockets at a 'splash-target' raft towed six hundred feet astern. One by one the Venoms and Seahawks dived from about two thousand feet and let fly with bombs and rockets and cannon fire; very dramatic but initially few hits. And between sorties the ships guns were manned and fired as if at action stations. And one afternoon all aircrew summoned on the Flight Deck and issued with khaki trousers and shirts with rank-badges, and with either a .32 Wesley or Smith & Wesson .38 pistols and leg holsters, and shown how to fire them, shooting at fairground-silhouette type targets set-up on rear of the Flight Deck; this was all beginning to look suspiciously more serious than an ordinary 'exercise', but we were reassured that it was all part of an extensive communications exercise 'Operation Boathook' which was to begin sometime in October. We continued exercising our 'Alert Patrol' sorties now from just inside the Mediterranean, zigzagging along the northern Moroccan coast, and then onto Malta where we joined other Carriers; HMS Eagle, HMS Bulwark, light helicopter carriers HMS Ocean and HMS Theseus, and four cruisers, a Destroyer, and two French Naval aircraft carriers, and although it became too obvious that something important was in the wind we were still kept in the dark; yet strangely nobody seemed particularly bothered!

Despite all of this frenetic activity the Wardroom still managed to celebrate Trafalgar Day- the 21st of October in splendid Royal Naval fashion; we dressed for our Banquet Dinner as if our main activities were merely routine, and entertained Captains from our sister-ships, as Albion had now become the Flag-ship of the enterprise, whatever that might be, commanded by a Vice-Admiral.

Albion's Chaplain, the Rev. Jim Sharpe included Nelson's own prayer in the Grace, which invited other private thoughts and speculations of what might be in store for us.

"May the great God, whom I worship, grant to my country and for the benefit of Europe in general, a great and glorious victory: and may no misconduct, in any one, tarnish it: and may humanity after victory be the predominant feature in the British fleet.

For myself individually, I commit my life to Him who made me and may His blessing light upon my endeavours for serving my country faithfully.

To Him I resign myself and the just cause which is entrusted to me to defend.

Amen. Amen. Amen."

(Prayer of Vice Admiral Horatio Lord Nelson off Cape Trafalgar, 21 October 1805)

The following day all three Carriers refuelled from the Fleet Tanker just off Malta, and surrounded by our escorting frigates, now we looked very much like an armada, especially from the air. And at last all aircrew were informed that we were to engage in real hostilities, to destroy the Egyptian Air force as part of 'Operation Musketeer', which we knew nothing about. So we were going to War after all, but the rest of the ship's crew were still kept guessing and were not informed almost until the final moments of our first strike!

I couldn't understand the reasons for this intense secrecy for it would have been impossible for anyone on board to make contact with anyone ashore, and anyway, there were plenty of war-like activities going on for all observers to see. All aircraft were being prepared for combat and painted with yellow and black identification stripes encircling the wings and around the rear fuselage, and long-range fuel tanks were fitted to our Skyraiders, and real live bombs and rockets and other aircraft ammunition was being transferred from holds deep in the lower parts of the ship, and stored just below the Flight Deck for ready use.

So when the Captain finally addressed the whole ship's crew with his announcement, the immediate response was relief and enthusiastic excitement, and 'Radio Albion' played uplifting patriotic music that evening with resonances of a previous war. For us of 'C Flight' our CAP's, (Combat Air Patrols) would not take us into any real danger and it was unlikely that we would even get a glimpse of any action; but war was in the air and all energies were directed at the enemy, whoever they might be.

SUEZ THEATRE OF WAR

As we arrived in our 'Combat Zone', a hundred or so miles north of Egypt; the Captain announced over the Tannoy that he had received a signal from the Commander-in Chief Mediterranean, to All Ship's Companies:

"We are now to carry out the operations for which you have trained and prepared with such spirit and enthusiasm. I am very proud to have such a large fleet under my command manned by a highly efficient and cheerful team of officers, ratings and Royal Marines. I have full confidence that you will carry out your duties with the same determination and courage for which the Royal Navy is famous, and that we shall with other Services and our French allies bring these operations to a successful conclusion. May all go well with you."

There was a brief moment of silence throughout the ship, then along passageways and mess decks and in the Hangars, and on the Flight Deck there was a pandemonium of cheers ringing out as if there had been some contagious message of celebration, but there was also the smell of fear in the air; we were sailing into the unknown!

Each Carrier is protected by a Cordon of Frigates; and there are also British submarines maintaining a lookout for possible enemy submarine attacks. Two ancient Egyptian Motor-Torpedo Boats which approached the Fleet had been dispatched by our Seahawks; but there were also constant irritations from American ships and aircraft which kept straying into our declared 'theatre of war' and which required constant warnings that we were prepared to send a 'shot across their bows' if necessary. During one of my CAPs I was approached by an American Skyraider from one of their Carriers, the pilot flew alongside me for a brief moment, grinning, and saluted me American –style and peeled off before I was able to report the incident. During debriefing we found out that there had been several 'heated exchanges' between the British and French Task Force commanders and the commander of the American Sixth Fleet with its two Carriers ; the USS Coral Sea and USS Randolf, operating in waters around Cypress; they were obviously keeping an eye on us and sometimes we picked them up on our Radar as 'enemy aircraft'.

During these last minute preparations there were several accidents, which cast a cloud of despondency among our aircrews. A catapult on HMS Eagle had failed during a launch and the Sea Hawk on the Cat failed to accelerate to the required speed to provide sufficient momentum and lift for flight, and ditched over the Port Bow. Fortunately the pilot was able to extricate himself from his sinking aircraft and the ship's steersman took immediate action and steered the ship to starboard allowing the pilot to be picked up by the 'safety helicopter'.

It had never occurred to us relatively new pilots that a catapult might ever fail to work, as most of us considered Deck-landings our only danger; but now we were required to reconsider our tactics in an event of catapult failure; and this was beginning to bother me. Sometimes I would replay my 'ditching-procedures' over and over as I tried to get to sleep, as it had become yet one more concern when preparing for a catapult launch! Some of these thoughts would also return when there was nothing pressing during a sortie, especially if I was over-flying Albion; and occasionally I would get irrelevant random thoughts such as; thinking bizarrely about such things as the 'energies' consumed by men and machines in sustaining all the activities required to drive the ship, and of the daily lives of what amounted to a small floating village; and thinking about this, it was probably me needing something to worry about, or perhaps trying to grasp the impossible-to-grasp bigger picture, and how I now thought I fitted into this new way of life, and way of being, and this floating metal village; distilling unbelievable amounts of sea water, for drinking, cooking and washing; and dozens of cooks baking thousands of loaves of bread and cooking hundreds of meals three times a day, and others; every day, laundering clothes, etc. for nearly two thousand men, amazingly, all like clockwork; and yet we take it all for granted as we did the impossible thought of a catapult failing to function correctly! And now we were battle ready; taking on an enemy we knew almost nothing about!

I could see the rapid build-up of ships and aircraft during my next daily CAPs, especially the numbers of RAF aircraft arriving in Cyprus; the huge Valiant Bombers, Canberra fighter-bombers, Hawker-Hunters, reconnaissance aircraft, and transports; the airspace above Cyprus was full of aircraft day and night, and besides this there were also high-altitude American Lockheed U-2 spy-planes flying from their Turkey airbase and occasional US fighters poking their noses in; during this last week of October it had become a virtual flying circus!

By the 31st we were on constant alert; and there had already been several false alarms. On one occasion two RAF Hunters intercepted two US Navy Banshees, which were picked up on our radar as possible enemy aircraft, and chased-off. RAF Canberra's were also flying reconnaissance sorties, penetrating Egyptian airspace and feeding us with up to date intelligence, while our Skyraiders and those of 849 Squadron 'A- Flight from HMS Bulwark, and French Naval 'Avengers' from their Carriers were conducting anti-submarine patrols and keeping an eye on movements of Egyptian naval vessels.

In our last minute briefing we were told that during the night of the 31st of October RAF bombers from Malta and Cyprus had raided targets along the Canal; Airfields at Cairo West, Almaza, Kabrit, Abo Sueir, and Inchas, with the intention of putting these Egyptian Air Force airfields out of action and destroying Egypt's Air Force aircraft.

Thursday 1st November 1956.

On the morning of the 1st November I was first on the catapult ready for a dawn launch at 0500 for my first CAP sortie and just prior to the launching of 36 Sea Hawks and Sea Venoms from Albion, Bulwark and Eagle. I was circling the combat zone at 8000 feet as the Sea Venoms and Sea Hawks were launched, and as the sun came up, casting its deep rosy glow, and long shadows across the theatre of war, as it must have done down the centuries; for these waters have witnessed some of the most famous sea battles of western history, and here was I observing and participating in possibly yet another, albeit small, historical chapter without really understanding the shenanigans that had brought me there.

But this was the start of our assault of the airfields, and to take control of Egyptian air-space above the canal, but I heard over the R/T that the high-level bombing by the RAF had not been as effective as expected, and very soon I gathered that some of the targets for the Hawks and Venoms had completely disappeared, and that the Egyptians had flown most of their aircraft to surrounding friendly countries for safe-keeping, but that there were still plenty of quality aircraft left behind; Russian supplied MIGs etc, and these were attacked by our jets with three inch rockets and destroyed. My role, with others that day was to provide radar air cover for the fleet, keeping watch for possible attacks from enemy aircraft, so I witnessed the continuous comings and goings of our Sea Venoms and Sea Hawks, and Wyverns from Bulwark, and the Corsairs and other French aircraft from the French Carriers. To call it a circus is not to disparage it but to highlight its remarkable 'choreography', and my admiration for the precision required to launch and recover so many aircraft efficiently demonstrated the effectiveness of our, what seemed to be such brief, preparations!

My pattern that day was to cover our three Carriers and the French Carriers with the rest of the Flotilla with our usual triangular flight plan, which took us just over the Egyptian and Syrian coast, so we were able to observe some of the destruction of the targets along the canal as well as the Egyptian coastal defences, as they were attacked. I maintained an altitude of between 18,000 and 20,000 feet, keeping well above attacking aircraft, which were going in, one after another, very low! By mid-day it was like a cinematic battle scene; unreal to some extent, with the Venoms swooping down in shallow dives, as if waiting in-line to let-go their rockets, with plumes of black-smoke spurting up out of the low desert haze, indicating hits on fuel bowsers or freshly fuelled aircraft; but all with very little Egyptian resistance. But there was still vehicle traffic moving slowly along the main roads inland, and spasmodic small-arms firing from the taller buildings in the town, but nothing capable of resisting our attack.

I observed the launches of our jets in waves and the recovery after they had completed their sorties, and finally joined the end of the queue to recover.

(*I recorded these thoughts during my de-briefing.*)

That evening I heard some of the accounts of the attacks from the jet squadron crews; it seems there was a little resistance from the enemy, only some feeble anti-aircraft fire; but all targets had been accounted for, with parked-aircraft and hangars destroyed and left burning in flames.

There was no real time for relaxation; all aircrew I chatted with between flights already seemed tired, and the aircraft maintenance crews had been working round the clock and had lost their initial enthusiasm for the fight; the rest of the ship operated in its machine-like fashion, and occasionally I would overhear questions from all quarters, about the reasons for the war beyond resisting the Egyptians 'nationalising' of the Canal. But as far as I understood it, we were simply defending our property; as stupidly simple as that might seem!

Radio Albion was blaring it's Records-Request for the ship, and even played the Hallelujah Chorus, sung at full belt by the Mormon Tabernacle Choir; I recorded my brief thoughts on this as: 'It takes all sorts!'

Ken Evans

Friday 2nd November 1956

Our first sorties were launched before dawn, at 0345. Albion launched two Skyraiders as part of our CAP, which now also included Sea Hawks from HMS Bulwark as a precaution against possible air attacks by Egyptian or other enemy aircraft. Even at this early hour there was already plenty of activity in the air; besides the continuous waves of Sea Hawks, Sea Venoms and Wyverns from the British Carriers there were Corsairs and Avengers from the two French Carriers; La Fayette and Arromanches. There was plenty of distance between our Carriers, but we were aware of their programmes, and we could hear the sounds of their sorties being launched, and once I was airborne, once again I had a ring-side seat, an Ariel -view, which had its own beauty as the first dawn light again cast its long red shadows across the dark sea.

There was also the continuous commentary over the R/T as the various returning flights were reporting damage to their aircraft. At last there was some resistance and anti-aircraft flak, some of it scoring hits on our aircraft. The RAF and French Air Force bombers were usually too high for the Egyptian gunners to reach, but air attacks by the Carrier Strike squadrons were attacking from low-level steep dives, and pulling out after delivering their rockets and bombs, and making their get-away at almost ground level. So low in fact that some of the damage to aircraft was caused by shrapnel from exploding targets; in one instance shrapnel pierced the cockpit floor of a Sea Venom and severely injured the Observer-Navigator; and there were several incidents where cockpit canopies were shattered by exploding anti-aircraft shells. But besides that there was relatively slight enemy damage; there were other accidents, including a Sea Hawk from 895 Squadron bottoming on No 4 wire on HMS Bulwark, at full throttle; ripping the arrester hook out which reduced flying speed somewhat but failed to stop the aircraft, and which slewed to the edge of the Flight Deck and went over the port bow, breaking- apart on hitting the sea, and sinking instantly with the loss of the young pilot. The French also lost a Corsair, which went over the side after the pilot misjudged his landing, and in attempting a 'Bolter" he opened up the throttle so rapidly that the aircraft flipped on its back as it veered away from the Flight Deck and crashed into the sea. But fortunately on this occasion the pilot was clear of the cockpit before it sank, and was picked up by the Carrier's Plane- guard helicopter within minutes. It seems that the older prop-driven aircraft are just slightly more buoyant than the new Jets, giving perhaps a few more seconds afloat, which makes all the difference between death and survival; a very sobering thought for the Jet aircrews.

The targets for Day-Two were mainly parked enemy aircraft and airfield installations, but there was a new one at Huckstep Barracks, just east of Cairo, where there were large numbers of armoured vehicles which appeared to be prepared for action, and by early afternoon, the last 75 sorties of the day were directed at the destruction of this armour, which somewhat oddly had been lined-up nicely for easy destruction, by low-level rocketing and strafing. The total number of sorties flown from our three British Carriers; HMS Eagle, HMS Albion and HMS Bulwark that day was a record 314 sorties which destroyed more than 50 Egyptian aircraft, and a similar number of aircraft Hangers and other maintenance installations, and more than a thousand armoured vehicles parked at Huckstep Camp. During the hours of darkness the RAF took over, and continued to bomb Luxor air-base and roads alongside the Canal. I myself had flown three sorties that day, and by the end of the day I felt washed-out!

After debriefing I showered and changed, and worked myself forward, along passage-ways, up and down ladders, through mess-decks and other strange flats and compartments to the Forecastle, properly called the foc'sle, which on the Albion is on the same level as the Quarterdeck, but at the opposite end of the ship; and the only two parts of the ship with traditionally-scrubbed wooden decks, and with that salty- smell of the sea.

The foc'sle has all the mechanisms for lowering and raising the giant anchors, and has massive bollards through which giant anchor-chains run, but my interest was the small platform jutting out above the centre-line of the ship which is intended for a linesman to take physical soundings with a knotted line when manoeuvring in shallow waters. I had spotted this small platform whilst circling the ship and was curious what it would be like to stand there, and look down as the ship ploughed her way through a choppy sea. And in the half-light of an orange sunset I stood there on that platform, alone looking ahead, viewing the waves as if I am myself an imaginary figurehead, and beneath me several playful porpoises twisting and diving through the moving waters being driven by the energy of the sharp edge of this mighty tub.

I could feel the piercingly cold spray on my face and the wind in my hair, and my shirt getting soaked, but the sheer exhilaration of feeling detached from it all after nearly a whole day wedged in my cockpit was like flying without wings. I could look down through the metal bars of the flimsy platform and sense myself walking on air or water, for how long I don't know, but even when I felt chilled to the bone I didn't want to let go.

Later I had to change for dinner, trussed up like a turkey or more like a penguin, but even that is something one gets used to!

There was a strange atmosphere of apprehension in the Wardroom as if a bubble was about to burst, and I probed a little but no one was forthcoming. I disappeared as soon as Dinner was finished and went back to my cabin to jot down my usual scribbles of what had been happening, but besides what I see, hear and think; it is impossible to dig any deeper. We haven't seen any newspapers since we arrived on-board, and whatever is communicated at higher levels is not passed down so we carry on until we finish our tasks; in typical proper Naval Fashion.

Saturday 3rd November

Albion withdrew north, beyond the Battle Zone, we needed to refuel and replenish, but Eagle and Bulwark's aircraft continued to maintain the attack of targets along the canal; French Corsairs attacked other targets including Radar installations. We picked up R/T transmissions from HMS Eagle's 830 Squadron of Wyverns; one of the Wyverns had been hit by anti-aircraft Flack, and the pilot was forced to escape over the coast and successfully ejected and had managed to inflate his dinghy, only to provide a more visible target for shore-line batteries. Fortunately there were sufficient Sea Hawks at hand to provide protective cover for the downed pilot, and to wipe-out the shore-based gun-emplacements while the rescue helicopter was making its way to pick him up.

From what we could make out from the intercom the jets were running out of targets, and were now flying reconnaissance sorties looking for possible other things to hit, including military vehicles and armoured tanks, which of course included their personnel.

After our refueling and replenishment, which included several large bags of mail, we returned to Battle Stations, and Eagle and the French Carriers took our place, withdrawing for their re-fuelling, and by nightfall, all three of our British Carriers were back on station and ready to renew action.

But when we are not night-flying, the ship is almost completely 'blanked –out, with the minimum number of navigation lights; almost too-small to be seen; port and starboard lights and similar-sized fore and aft white navigation lights. From the Flight Deck I can see the other ships of our Flotilla spread-out, similarly lit, but from our ship insufficient light to create any reflections from the sea; the sensation is that we moving silently and slowly forward, suspended in total darkness, and aft in our wake a pale hint of jade-green 'wash' trailing into the distance. In these conditions we are making, perhaps, no more than ten or twelve knots, with hardly any sense of rocking-movement, but as soon as I enter the 'Island', dazzled by the light and noise, and warm-smell of the ship's interior life! With Radio Albion banging-out its cacophony of Rock and Roll, and the rattling roar of the ventilation truncking and other subsidiary vibrations.

Sunday 4th November

We were again at Battle Stations but there was a lull, and it seemed that we were taking a breather and pulling ourselves together preparing for the next phase of the operation when it was unexpectedly announced over the Tannoy that 'Divine Service' would take place on the Flight Deck at 1100 hours. I hadn't expected this, but I had seen the Ship's Chaplain several times popping his head out of the 'island' door to the Flight Deck and assumed that he was just showing his face, but I later gathered that he had reminded the Captain that we should keep on good terms with the Almighty, just to be on the safe side.

Attendance at religious services is to some extent voluntary, but there are times when Ratings and others are ordered to attend, and on this occasion there were more than a hundred or so who had made the effort to change into number two's (a second best uniform) and to stand on the stern of the Deck, and lustily sing hymns and bowing their heads in prayer as the Royal Marine Band accompanied them, with me among them. The Chaplain reminded us that these seas are full of the remains of dead sailors and that we have an obligation to remember them, for we can never know when we will be called to join them. Ordinary sailors it seems, despite their reputation for occasional wild behavior ashore, are surprisingly religious in a primitive kind of way, believing in fate and luck; perhaps this is the traditional mark of the sea-farer, for when the sea is angry even a large Carrier is tossed about like a toy-boat, and there is an age-old natural inclination to refer to the words of the Sailor's hymn; "*for those in peril on the seas*".

Less than half an hour later, after the Chaplain had given us his Blessing, the mood on the Flight Deck quickly changed back to action-stations; aircraft were being armed, and aircrew were being strapped in and lining up for launching on the Catapult. My CAP included reconnaissance along the coast searching for small Egyptian Navy vessels, MTBs and other make-shift gun-boats that might present a threat to the flotilla. From above the coast I could also see our jets heading in the direction of Cairo West, and my own sweep took me along the coast and coves beyond Port Said where I was able to see some of the damage further in-land, and again the plumes of black smoke spiraling into the sky, like billowing dark fountains. On my second arm, I turned north, climbing to 20,000 feet as far as Tel Aviv and then descending to about 5,000 for a pass over the American Carriers which were heading in the direction of our Flotilla; they must have known that I would be flying across their bows; I could see arms waving from their Island. As I was turning onto my third vector I heard over the intercom from one of our Sea Venoms that the pilot had spotted several small surface vessels, and was on his run-in to strafe them, and whilst firing his cannon, he describing the face of one of their gunners trying to down his aircraft, but when he looked back the boat was ablaze and out of control. I continued to fly above the flotilla, along the hundred mile, or so, arm of a triangle, then turning left 120 degrees which would give us a three hundred mile radar cover above our Carriers' the air was full of aircraft striking shore- batteries and gun emplacements; with no time at all, at moments like this, to think about anything else other than what is happening, moment by moment.

Flying CAP Patrols when there is a lot of activity means that I have to operate most of the time at a higher altitude, around 20, 000 feet, from where everything looks like an intense battle-ground; there were several waves of Sea Hawks from Albion striking gun emplacements along the coast and I watch the flak as the heavier guns were defending their shore-line; it was hot work and continued into the afternoon as I prepared to return to my ship, back to Albion and recovered back on-board. My crew in the back always jokingly complimenting me on 'another good-landing'; I rarely need to bolt and go round again, and despite the increasing number of sorties I'm not so sure that my 'deck landings' have become any easier, or lighter! But in these sea conditions the Flight-Deck was relatively stable and the visuals were clear; all I had to do was to trim my cab to maintain a proper approach speed, line-up the lights on the Mirror, hold the glidescope ball central, and cut when the Deck Officer signals.

During de-briefing we learned that Anglo-French invasion fleet was on its way from Malta making ready for an assault landing tomorrow, and that the strafing of shore batteries had been part of a softening-up operation, so what I had observed was at last looking like real war, rather than a Turkey-Shoot of tame-aircraft on the ground.

Monday 5th of November

It was another early launch for me and the whole of the squadron, 'C Flight' had all four Skyraiders airborne before 0700 hours, patrolling back and forth the invasion fleet from Malta, with HMS Theseus and HMS Ocean, both helicopter Carriers in the lead, apparently with assault troops, including Royal Marine Commandoes preparing to attack Port Said, to coincide with the airborne invasion by British and French paratroops flown from Cyprus. So at last this was beginning to look like a real invasion; Sea Hawks, Sea Venoms and Wyvern already clearing the Coastal defences along the coast as dawn was breaking, and then moving further inland, down the canal to clear any Egyptian straggling defensive movements.

Albion's aircrews only learned that there was to be an airborne invasion during our very brief 'Briefing' that morning, as the operation was being controlled from Cyprus, at least initially, and our efforts of the previous four days were essentially preparation for that. All I understood from that was that we were securing airspace and providing Air-Cover, and clearing any 'resistance' immediately prior to and during the Parachute Drop.

From my perch I could see the Carrier Task Force moving closer to the Egyptian coast as the RAF Valletta's and Hastings troop-carriers approached the coast at about 700 feet, discharging their paratroops in one continuous stream of white mushrooms over the Dropping Zone at Gamil Airfield. Up until this point Operation Musketeer had still seemed like an exercise, but now there were British and French soldiers occupying Egyptian territory and defending it as their own. At last I could really believe that this was war, and I was part of it, a very small part but a part never the less! Then helicopters arrived with more troops, and groups of paratroops spread out in all directions, some encountering hostile enemy gun-fire. I could see a gun emplacement on top of a very high building more or less in the centre of Port Said town, which later I learned was the Egyptian Headquarters, controlling the defence of the whole region and which was quickly 'neutralised, by an onslaught of our rockets delivered by our 895 Squadron's Sea Hawks.

Stories were beginning to emerge of casualties; the intercom was abuzz with calls for air-cover as both British and French paratroops encountered pockets of resistance, with Egyptian guns firing at paratroops as they were landing. The French had been dropped further down the canal near the al-Raswa bridges with the intention of controlling the main road to Suez, which would in effect, with occupation of Port Said, controlling both ends of the canal. From the number of calls for air cover from the French, it was obvious that there was more resistance their end, and they were directing their own air support; mainly Corsairs from their Carriers-Arromanches and La Fayette for protection. (Actually prop-aircraft are much better for supporting ground troops; jets are too fast, and Corsairs are made for the job!)

Mid-morning as I was preparing to return to Albion; there were several waves of French Corsairs back and forth between their Carriers and the two target areas, and by the time I had completed my de-briefing, I heard that the French had made a further drop of 500 paratroops over the Port Fuad area, closing-off both sides of the canal, and by mid afternoon the Egyptian High Command were offering their surrender. But it was not clear if this had been accepted, because there had apparently been 'discussions' between Russia and our Allied governments, and apparently also the American government had complained about our war. This news had been passed down from the 'highest' officials in London, which had also hinted at a 'cease-fire' without any detailed explanations.

By the end of the day, Sea Hawks and two of our Skyraiders maintained CAPs as the Carrier Force withdrew north for the night. I was able to make my way to the Foc'sle again to stand on the small over-hanging platform over-looking the bow-waves billowing up as the ship ploughed her way through the dark sea; plankton sparkling in the troughs with porpoise weaving playfully back and forth in our bow-waves. In the darkness there was nothing else to see but the lights from the rest of the flotilla, besides these it seemed we were all alone in the darkness of night.

Radio Albion had changed mood, with Elvis singing 'Since my Baby left me', and 'Hound Dog', obviously the flavor of the moment!

My 'Flight Log' giving no indication of our changing thoughts about this operation, but today I think I saw some bodies floating in the sea near the shore-line; fathers and sons perhaps and had been wondering when they might be recovered, or if they would be left to rot there, unclaimed and unknown!

Tuesday 6th November.

All of Albion's aircrews, and most probably those of the other Carriers, knew that this was to be the big day, a mini-version of World War Two's 'D-Day' landings, and by 0230 hours the Flight Deck was busily moving aircraft around in preparation for an early morning launch. The combined Carrier Strike Force had moved closer to the Egyptian coast and was now battling against heavy winds and driving rain; we were now in the centre of a turbulent thunderstorm, the wind whipping-up a very choppy sea; unpleasant for us, but worse for the landing craft preparing for a dawn attack.

As I stepped out of the Island onto the Flight Deck, I was nearly blown off my feet by the heavy 40 knots head-wind; but the Flight Deck teams were jauntily weaving in and out of the sections of Sea Hawks and Venoms and preparing for the first launches. I could hear and see the distant flashes from our Destroyer's heavy guns, which had moved nearer the coast and were already pounding coastal defences, and clearing the beaches designated as landing areas, and I saw several waves of RAF Venoms coming in low from the sea and taking it in turns to fire their rockets into an array of targets on the coast and further in-land in the town.

I had been launched at 0515, and was over flying the beaches as the Royal Marines landed. Our Sea Hawks were also over-flying as they arrived, strafing small-gun emplacements, which had been rapidly assembled as a 'welcoming party'. The whole scene was rapidly changing with each circular pass we made; the next time we passed the beach it was covered with Centurion tanks, with our marines moving from the beach to higher ground. Further along the coast French paratroop were also landing, and helicopters were flying back and forth between HMS Ocean, a helicopter Carrier, and the water-front, where there was intense fighting with Egyptian troops; and already I was hearing emergency calls for helicopters to move casualties back to the Carriers for medical attention. Considering the speed at which everything was happening, it was surprising that there weren't more casualties.

By mid-day the coastal airfield at Gamil, to the east of Port Said, had been secured by paratroops, and was being cleared for use as a landing strip. Fortunately the runways were still serviceable and most of the buildings around the control tower were intact, but the mains water supply had been sabotaged and the troops were running out of drinking water. I was re-called to Albion with two other Skyraiders, and as soon as we had landed on, drop-tanks were fitted to our aircraft. It had been proposed that we fill them with fresh water. These drop-tanks had never been used for fuel or any other liquids, so they should have been clean, but after being fitted under the main-plane (wings) and flushed out several times the ship's Medical Officer tested the water and advised against it. At this point there were several suggestions, and the most straight-forward and simplest was to send canned beer from our on-board NAAFI supplies. Removing one of the Observers seats and some of the Radar equipment from the rear cockpit of Boss's aircraft, it was possible to load the rear fuselage compartment with a 1,000 cans, but this wasn't deemed enough for the 'Wooly-Heads' (Royal Marine Commandoes and Paratroopers), so both rear seats were removed from my cab, and more cans of beer and other 'liquids' were loaded, and the Boss and I were quickly sent to Gamil, where one of the runways had been cleared for our arrival; some of the beer cans were still chilled when unloaded and distributed to the troops. We had a 'mooch-round', and while we were there several RAF Valettas arrived from Cyprus with Medics and medical supplies, but not adequately able to deal with one badly wounded soldier who was immediately flown to Cyprus. We also were able to ferry three wounded soldiers back to Albion with us when we returned on-board. I could see from the numbers of wounded paratroopers that the so-called skirmishes had been heavily resisted, and some of the paratroopers had been fired on as they were descending during their parachute Drop. Many of the less seriously wounded casualties were ferried back to HMS Eagle and Theseus, and French casualties had been picked up by helicopters and brought to Gamil and then flown on to Cyprus. By late afternoon the helicopters were operating a shuttle service ferrying fresh water and medical supplies, and beer and even freshly-made sandwiches for the troops, and returning with casualties.

We heard over the R/T that a RAF Canberra had been shot down with the loss of aircrew, and that a Sea Hawk from HMS Eagle had been hit and the pilot ejecting over hostile territory. Thankfully there were several Sea Hawks from the same squadron in the vicinity, and these were able to report the position and to cover the downed pilot for a while, who apparently had already attracted attention from unidentified ground troops. One of the French Corsair pilots who had also observed the wounded Sea Hawk, and had circled above the downed pilot, and swooped down to attack approaching Egyptian tanks, and three other Corsairs joined in the cover, eventually a Whirlwind rescue helicopter from Eagle arrived and picked-up the pilot. From what I later learned, every airborne naval pilot had been listening in to the drama over the R/T. For the rest of the afternoon French and British aircraft were being called-in to deal with the heavy ground fire around Port Said from Egyptian defenders; and Carriers were still launching aircraft as the sun went down.

Since returning on board from Gamil I had been on-call and ready for another sortie if needed, but I had also heard on the grapevine that political pressures on the British government had 'forced' a 'Cease Fire', to take effect from midnight, but as this hadn't yet been announced over the Tannoy most of us who had heard the 'Buzz' took it with a pinch of salt. The Sea Hawks and Venoms were already armed and ready for launching, but a pall of disappointment had settled over the ship as if our enthusiasm had been dowsed and drained away, and I think it was this that had led to the decision for one more 'last' strike before night-fall. The Sea Hawks of 800 Squadron were launched for a final strike on Navy House, which in former times had been the administrative HQ for Royal Navy ships in the Eastern Mediterranean, but now stuck-out like a sore-thumb of Egyptian resistance.

I had often admired this beautiful white building and had used it as a 'location point', and had flown over it many times, and in my mind I had seen it not so much as a symbol of our imperial past, but as a little bit of English stability, a sign of our role as guardians and protectors of freedom of the seas maintaining the canal as an international waterway. But now Navy House was occupied by a political group of 'squatters' who wanted to 'seize' the canal, and to my mind, set themselves up as the new owners of Navy House. So for some of us this target had come to symbolize what we had been fighting for; not just for the possession of a building but for principals which were somehow contained in the elegance of its design and its purpose, and which now had been commandeered as a 'gun emplacement'.

Later that evening, accounts of the 'last sortie' were shared and toasted in the Wardroom. Our own 800 squadron and 899 from Eagle had lined up to take their turn to attack the building, diving from 2000 feet, aiming their rockets through the many veranda-windows and clearing the emplacements from the flat roof. One by one the opposing gun-fire from each of the windows and verandas had ceased, and flames licked the front of the building and the roof; the building had burned-out overnight. By the following morning it had become a blackened shell, with less than twenty survivors of it's fifty or so defenders. And at midnight the cease-fire actually came into force, instigated mainly by our 'friends of that special relationship' in America; but we had just in time managed to deny the enemy the satisfaction of owning and desecrating the dignity of our Navy House.

The following morning all aircrews were briefed that we were to maintain operational readiness; that we were on stand-by, but our Carriers would withdraw from our battle zone to await further developments. Most of us took this news as confirmation of what we had been thinking anyway; we had achieved what we had set out to do, and we had finished the job; for that was all it was to us - just another job; and further developments would take us to other places. We maintained a reduced schedule of daily sorties and used the rest of the time to recuperate and reflect on our performance, but for me, apart from being able to observe some of the drama of the jet squadron's attacks, my own protective sorties had been virtually the same as practice flights except for the numbers of aircraft which appeared on our radar screens.

Albion's Captain addressed the whole ship's Company over the Tannoy, thanking us for our efforts, and read us similar messages from the Fleet's Commander-in-Chief, but obviously there was no reference to the political background to the cease-fire, and if there had been it would have been of little interest to us. Somehow that part of the picture seemed too distant from us, and after a while at sea even what is happening at home seems so disconnected that we seem to live only for the actual moment! Whilst we are preparing for our 'launch' that is where our thoughts are, and once in the air we are searching the skies for enemy aircraft, and the same with each of our duties. There is hardly any time for stray thoughts or consideration of what is happening in the rest of the world; our thoughts rarely stretch beyond the bounds of our mother-ship, and while we are in the air, our Cab's crew's concerns shrink to the limits of our aircraft, Skyraider Z320, of 849 Squadron, 'C' Flight.

But now there is time for other things and other thoughts. The ship is to visit Cyprus for a few days and hopefully there will be a chance to go ashore, and for some a chance to celebrate their little victories! We anchored some three miles off the Bay of Limassol, clear of the busy shipping routes, and Shore-Leave arrangements were announced over the Tannoy. The ship's crew (proper) is divided into 'watches' which means that only a quarter of the ships compliment are allowed shore-leave at any one time, and this is carefully regulated. Officers are free to go ashore if they are not required for any ship's duties, and I noted from the Roster that I am 'Duty-Officer' for tomorrow, which could mean that I might be Manning one of the Quarter-Deck points, where sailors (ratings) go and return on-board from their shore-leave, and are checked out and checked back on-board after their 'Run Ashore'. I've done this before and there is a little bit of ceremony attached to this; as Officer of the Watch, I am in effect responsible for the Ship's Good Order and Naval Discipline, which means that each man leaving the ship has to salute me and request permission to leave the ship, and I in return salute him and check that his dress is 'correct', and if I choose I can send him back to his mess-deck to 'tidy himself up', this is rarely necessary, but when they return on-board it can be a different matter; fortunately I have four or more Regulation Branch (RN Police) Ratings to assist me with any defaulters.

Or I could be responsible for organizing one of many Work-Parties, which could mean almost anything; Parties for loading provisions from boats, painting-ship parties, scrubbing the Quarter-Deck, polishing Brass, etc, etc. Frequently these 'jobs' are pointless and meaningless, but the work-parties are there to be employed and a Duty Officer is there to ensure that even the pointless jobs are completed to the same standards as necessary jobs; it's part of the logic of RN tradition! But the worst duty of all for any Duty Officer is taking charge of a Shore Patrol, which usually includes restraining and arresting 'Drunken Sailors'.

I did this once when I was in Malta, and felt out of my depth in more ways than one when I had ordered two huge Ratings to arrest a super-strong fearless sailor who wanted to kill me for some reason. Even after being at sea for a few weeks, some sailors seem to need to express their freedom from the constraints of ship-board life, and of heavy and dangerous work, through the time-honoured pursuits of 'wine women and song', and of defending their honour with fisty-cuffs. There is always bloodshed and I had to 'arrange' their arrest and transportation back to the ship; for them, back to their cage, whilst at the same time ensuring Admiralty Order and Good Naval Discipline in places where our ratings were congregating, whilst at the back of my mind my thoughts are that all I ever wanted to do was to fly planes off and onto aircraft carriers. And I picked-up-on the language of those shore-patrol sailors; whose favourite expression in those circumstances had been; "F*** this for a game of Sailors!" How eloquent I thought, a phrase that seemed to more than adequately capture the essence of the moment! (reference this book's title) and which still resonates with me when I'm carried back to those distant times, but no longer young, perhaps now re-cast by some as an old reprobate, not unlike blind Captain Cat, whose sense of humour, through and through, is that of jolly Jack Tar, and who sees all and knows all, and in some strange way, mourns all!

In the meantime I strolled around the, now relaxed, Flight-Deck, enjoying the gentler pace of work being done, and chatting with the crews from the jet squadrons, and our maintenance crews, who I rarely get the chance or time simply to pass the time of day, and talk about nothing in particular. Its moments like this that I realise how isolated we have all become; doing our jobs, almost machine-like, and only once in a while being able to enjoy chatting about nothing in- particular!

The general view about the Cease-Fire was that it had been a complicated decision beyond our reach, and that we had finished the job anyway and that we would probably get back home for Christmas, but it seems that it is not going to work out that way. We remained anchored in Limassol for only four days and we were up and away again, heading for Malta before I got round to thinking about going ashore, so I missed visiting Limassol, which apparently was no great loss.

But before we left Cyprus we were visited by and entertained Lt. General Sir Hugh Stockwell, one of the Commanders of the Suez Campaign, who also came up on the Flight Deck to meet and chat with aircrew and the Flight Deck crews, and was greeted by an impromptu squad of ratings, wearing their number twos back to front, and carrying a banner bearing the slogan, 'We're walking backwards to Christmas." (borrowed from the Goons), and the General instantly got the joke, and reversed his own cap. We were told later that he could 'snap' at this kind of silliness, but at this time he was howling with laughter at the sailor's jokes!

From what I could gather from various 'buzzes' doing their Rounds, the Carrier Force was expected to remain in the Med for a while, perhaps as some kind of guarantee that we were still around and showing the flag, and before the ship reached Malta, as usual all four of C Flight's Cabs flew off to Hal Far Air Base with the Jet Squadrons, probably so that we could still operate if necessary whilst our ship was anchored in Valletta Harbour.

RONNIE'S BAR

HMS Falcon at Hal Far is the Royal Navy's Mediterranean
Air Station, and was probably one of the first Fleet Air Arm's
first own Air Stations anywhere in the world; and retained
many of the original accommodation buildings but still
resembled a primitive worn-out RAF World-War II airfield,
with very basic living accommodation, an old Control Tower
and antique-style aircraft Hangars; but it became more lively
now with squadrons from Eagle and Bulwark to keep us
company. At the far end of the main Runway there was an
American contingent - a US Air Force squadron, flying
Neptune's, which were huge AEW (aircraft early warning
but more like Bombers) aircraft, doing more or less the same
job as our Skyraiders, but in considerably more luxurious
circumstances. The crews lived in specially designed pre-
fabricated building with all mod-cons, and even sported a
luxurious Mess, but best of all was their proximity to the
famous 'Ronnie's Bar' at the end of the runway; a large
and airy 'refreshments' palace resembling something out
of Hollywood Movies, (in other words –a large dilapidated
shack) which seemed to be continuously occupied by off-
duty American aircrew; eating, drinking and playing
pinball machines. I had heard a lot about this place before
I eventually braced myself to go there; apparently the main

appeal was the character Ronnie who first and foremost was a Raconteur, of rare charm and ability; he had a story for every conceivable situation, and as reputation had it, that if someone had a story about their black cat, he had one about an even blacker one!

Ronnie was as wide as he was short; built like a wrestler, and could rustle-up, as the Americans boasted, a 'real-steak' sandwich any time of day, or night, which I eventually tested and agreed was far superior to anything served in our Officer's Mess. He was also well-stocked with every conceivable 'liquor', mostly it seems from the local American PX Store, and he served ice-cold beer, and sported a giant American Juke Box loaded with the latest American records which played non-stop at full volume.

When I first tried Ronnie's, wearing my American Standard-Issue Navy leather flying jacket (a gift from my American class-mates from Penscola on gaining my wings) and sporting what was then termed a 'crew-cut', Ronnie's 'Girls' greeted me as if I were an American Flyer, and were stunned by my strange English accent and shyness, (I suppose I might claim it as my English reserve), which turned out to be a winning combination, (more about that later) One of the American Crew nick-named me 'Red' on account of the colour of my hair, which was soon picked up by the 'ladies', who failed to make the connection, and understand the reasons for the name! But the name stuck, and stayed with me when we returned back onboard our ship.

Whilst in Malta I was only required to fly one sortie a day, usually around the Maltese coastline, and in my free-time I got to enjoy the almost make-believe atmosphere of Ronnie's Bar, and also which, the non-stop playing of Elvis Presley, Fats Domino and Johnny Ray on the Juke-Box, had consequently impressed their words and rhythms in my head; I even learned to feed that great Wurlitzer-styled machine with my spare change and occasionally exchanged wicked glances with some of the local 'beauties' who were Ronnie's constant guests, or of his American 'Buddies', who hung around the glitzy music machine, moving clumsily to the music.

The American aircrews knew that we flew Skyraiders and several of them reminisced with us their own experiences of flying 'Spads', as they lovingly called them; a few of them 'Nam-Veterans' who had claimed to have 'downed' Russian Migs and survived because 'Spads' were lucky Cabs, but they thought our AD-3W's – Guppies, with their bulbous ray-domes were a 'Pansey's version', but even so still Skyraiders, and we were considered 'OK Limeys' because of this, especially when they learned how small our Flight-Decks were for Deck Landings; we pretending there was nothing to it!

Ronnie's Place was open all day and all night and the Neptune night-flying crews came in during the evening in their flying gear to top-up on beefsteak sandwiches and peanut and jam toasties for their sorties, and cracked jokes about going missing in action, or maybe not returning. Sometimes we would hear them taking-off and purposely making low-level passes over Ronnie's, either as a 'salute' to us or as a reminder of their 'connection' to the local bar-girls who were mostly wearing US Air Force Flight-Jackets and Baseball caps as their badges of affection or affiliation.

But before we left Malta, some of our crews had decided to visit the 'Gut' in Valetta; if for no other reason than at least to have witnessed it's existence. Actually it was vile! Almost everyone I met seemed to know of it, and its reputation, and I am sure that every British sailor of those times would have stories to tell; and for that reason alone, I agreed, it was worth a visit.

This very ancient street, called Straight Street, known to sailors as the 'Gut', was hardly a street, more a dark and narrow and steep lane, between tall buildings which could stand almost as a metaphor for Jolly Jack's descent from relative sanity to ruin, on his run-ashore after some time at sea. Almost every door was entrance to a Bar, with hideous misshapen worn-out Bar- Girls enticing passing sailors inside, as they tumbled down the cracked-uneven ancient flag-stones road. The din of music, some from Juke-Boxes, but also from pianos, with raucous singing, and the general hub-bub of Jolly-Jack's 'Wine, Women and Song, was ribald and wildly exciting. There were sailors bodies everywhere, being pulled and pushed into the Bars, sitting and lying drunkenly on the ground, heads popping from windows, all with the strong stench of urine and vomit, and the angry sounds of Bar-fights. Our little group walked in silence from the top to the bottom, and then climbed back up to relative calmness of Valletta's main shopping area; where for some strange reason I felt impelled to purchased a huge over-ripe water-melon; which I might have thought would be thirst-quenching back on-board, but which I eventually dropped into the ogg-wash whilst climbing up the gangway returning on-board.

CHRISTMAS

We thought we would be spending Christmas at Hal Far, but we re-joined our ship during mid December calling in at Messina, Sicily, where one of our Senior Officers arranged a skiing trip to mount Etna; a mad thing to do but one of the rare perks of serving in the RN! It was a brilliant surprise and for a whole day our group skied and lived the high-life as if we were wealthy tourists. Some of the other junior officers who stayed on-board relaxed in the restaurants and bars around Messina, and then we were off again, celebrating Christmas Day on board, with fun and games on the Flight Deck with a 'Beard' Competition and other mad sports-day events. I was still only shaving every other day, so I wasn't eligible for the competition.

The rating's mess-decks were strewn with hand-made paper-chains, and the food was real Christmas Fare, with Carols organized by the 'Bish' (ship's Chaplain) and something resembling a Pantomime, with a sailor's chorus in drag, performed one end of the Hangar, on the lowered Hangar Lift, and viewed from the Flight-Deck above; all, I aught to say, part of Royal Naval tradition! Jack Tar is very much a Jolly Fellow on such occasions, but when we return to normal routine, he awakes as if from a dream!

And Boxing Day should have been a return to that routine, but even before breakfast that morning, news had already travelled rapidly round the Mess-Decks and throughout the ship, that a young Petty Officer's body had been discovered hanging from a deck-head hook in a Caboosh, (a small paint-store); he had hanged himself during the night, apparently on learning that his wife had spent Christmas Day with his best friend and had wanted to leave him. There is no knowing how these 'buzzes' began, but whatever the real truth, they always seemed to do their rounds, gathering momentum and their own conviction and remaining as a kind of- after-thought. In these circumstances the deceased man's possessions are 'auctioned-off' to his shipmates, to raise money for his next-to-kin', but these auctions are not a true auctions; for a pair of socks might go for twenty or more pounds, only to be thrown back into the pile to be sold again! I heard that this auction raised more than two thousand pounds, despite the deep-felt ambivalence about the causes of his suicide.

His body was wrapped in his Admiralty-Issued thick canvas hammock, and sown up in the traditional manner, with the last stitch through his nose, and his body committed to the deep, sliding into the sea from a sloping-table on the Quarterdeck; and as he sank beneath the waves, the long silence punctuated by muted sobs. On these occasions even hardened seafarers weep!

We still had no idea when we would be heading for home and after a few more days replenishing at sea, which was now more hazardous in the exceptionally heavy weather, we zig-zagged on route to Marsaille; another unexpected visit, where we were invited to the French Naval Officers Mess, more or less as Brothers in Arms, where not only the cuisine and wine were superior to anything else, but also the female guests. But just as we were beginning to get our feet under the tables, we were again whisked away, back to Gibralter. I'm beginning to think that these short visits are one of the ways the Royal Navy imposes a form of celibacy as a means of maintaining their hold on their men's dependency, for in Naval parlance, 'The Puss' (colloquial term for Naval Purser) is mother and wife and the source of all basic needs!. Well not quite all!

And so to Gib, which is the entrance and exit to the Med and is now more of a stopping-off place than anything else; at least to the men it is the last shore-run before Pompey, a place to buy a few Rabbits (gifts for families at home), and a week there is a few days too much, but luckily for us 'the ship's Jimmy' had arranged a run-ashore to Tangiers (for Officers only) and limited to numbers using the Captain's Cutter to take us there, the ten miles or so across the Straits.

I had expected this to be a 'dignified' event, but it seems that the 'Jimmy-the-One' (Ship's 'First Lieutenant') knew Tangiers well, and had arranged a celebration Dinner for someone, (an old girl-friend I think) and we ended up after a short tour, in a sumptuous hotel overlooking the Straits, where there was plenty of wine, and women and song; (mostly Rugby songs :- 'one short one, one long one', etc.) and lots of high-jinks. But most memorably was the passing-around of a small mechanical novelty, which turned out to be a clockwork wanking machine. (I'm not kidding you!) We all had to guess it's purpose, and only the Ship's Chaplain guessed correctly, which led to some bizarre speculation. (We were all slightly pissed by then.) But even worse, another of the senior officers tried to sketch it, claiming that it was not beyond the ship's engineers capability to replicate it. Whether this project reached fruition, I have no idea! But it was a memorable run ashore; and we all managed to climb back onboard without serious injury. And so we were at last homeward-bound or so it seemed, but there was yet one more cruel twist; we were on our way home via Scotland where the Carrier- Fleet was to receive a Royal Review, in other words to entertain Her Royal Highness, The Queen, which we were informed by the Ship's Captain should be regarded as a compliment and honour. But before going to the Firth of Forth for that Review, we were to pay a visit to Trondheim, Denmark; partly as a way of killing time and as it turned out, also a sheltered anchorage, where we would be able to tidy-up the ship which was in need of some re-painting.

TRONDHEIM PAINTING PARTY

Almost as soon as we anchored the whole ship's company was organized into a Painting Party, including junior officers; which turned out to be a very unusual and strange life-experience. Aircraft Carriers have expansive areas of overhangs, which can only be accessed from huge metal-rope nets which are hung from the sides of the Flight –Deck, and pulled –in close to the concave sides of the ship with metal cables, and into which we, the painters had to scramble and climb like agile monkeys, which to me looked far more hazardous than making even a Deck –Landing in heavy weather. But we were all issued with dark-blue dungarees and white plimsolls and leather gloves, and shown how to scrape the surface- rust from the ship's sides and to apply paint using a peculiar long-handled brush with an angled round head of bristles, which was surprisingly effective. An undercoat of Red-Lead, followed by Battle Ship Grey; and we weren't just touching up the rusty bits but painting the whole ship, which in Norway in January, even in a sheltered harbor, was uncomfortably and bitterly cold! And because the palaver of climbing into the exact position took such a long time, we could not afford the time of frequently climbing back on-board to warm ourselves up, so after even a morning's work, we were frozen to the bone; but there was kind of comfort in the strange sense of camaraderie between officers and men, perhaps because firstly, in our overalls we all looked the same, and we were all subject to the same constraints of hard work and harsh conditions, and also with a fair amount of jibing (naval humour) from the work-hardened older ratings, which was usually also heart-warmingly funny, and surprisingly we made good progress!

Occasionally paint-pots and brushes would be dropped into the sea, usually accompanied by a 'Cheer' from the rest of the crew, and sometimes the ropes that were used to pull-in the nets would become loose, and a whole section would billow-out into the wind, like a loose spinnaker complete with clinging bodies swinging clear of the ship's sides, but someone would come to our rescue and pull back the nets and the 'bodies' would carry on painting as if nothing had happened. When building the Pyramids you lose all sense of time; it just passes, and while re-painting the hull of a Carrier we were too stiff with cold to go ashore at the end of the working day. But when the other sections of the ship were being renovated the massive Paint Parties were disbanded, and the Junior Officers were released back into their more usual duties, which for me were very few, so I did get ashore and see something of Trondheim City and enjoyed some pleasant meals in decent restaurants, and also entertained a few of the charming local ladies.

Concerning the ladies, we were sometimes introduced to at occasional Civic celebrations and then invited to private Parties, unfortunately one of the Sea Venom pilots and I fancied the same girl, (this keeps happening to me) and even worse, unknown to both of us she gave us her address, which later led to quite complicated misunderstandings between us. (a separate saga too intricate to relate)

After leaving Trondheim, Albion headed north, into the North Sea, almost to within the Artic Circle where the ship was sometimes tossed about like a toy-boat in some of the heaviest seas I had yet seen, and with waves sending their freezing spray over the Flight Deck; forty or more feet in the air. The aircraft on Deck were doubly secured to the deck with metal-rope harnesses, but still looked as if they might be blown away in the heavy ice-filled gales, and the ship heaved and rolled, and for several days everything was battened down; it being almost impossible to walk upright on the Flight-Deck. And I wondered why we were maintaining our course, as if the Helmsman had gone mad and was challenging all of the elements. (I can remember dreaming of the Flying Dutchman story that night.)

But when the gales slackened the Flight-Deck Crews heaved-to and were making ready in preparation to launch aircraft. It still seemed to me too dangerous for launching, and some of the jet pilots were expressing doubts about their willingness to fly in these conditions when there seemed no 'pressing' operational reason. And I knew that if there were to be Sorties, our Skyraiders would be first to launch; and then we were called for Briefing. In these conditions we had to don our Goon-suits; rubberized suits, which become waterproof when immersed, and we went through ditching procedures practice.

It was decided we were to launch and provide our usual AEW cover for the ship, and Venoms and Sea Hawks were to fly sorties, to test launching and recovery in 'severe

conditions'. In these high-wind conditions Skyraider wings
are locked in their folded position with large 'Jury-Struts',
which are like builder's heavy scaffolding tubes, and the
maintenance crews were having great difficulty in removing
them in the heavy wind; and the mechanic who helped me
into my cockpit mumbled something about 'madness', but
I had my helmet on and could hardy make-out what he was
saying, and then I was on the Cat, and throttling up. With
the ship heaving into a raging forty-plus knots headwind,
I could feel the movement of the ship through the seat of
my pants, and with each sudden gust the aircraft would be
thrown off the deck and to bounce back, the main-planes
(wings) shuddering with each fresh gust of wind. I made
myself ready in case I didn't clear the Deck, but I was
wheels-off well before the end of the Catapult track, and
climbing away as quickly as possible. I was followed by
the Boss in another Skyraider and as soon as he was clear
and also climbing, I 'OK-'d' him on the R/T, but he kept
repeating "Say Again!", his usual term for 'Repeat'; we were
still climbing and circuiting the ship, and as we completed
our 'Pass' at ten thousand feet, I heard over the R/T from
Carrier Flight Control that a Sea Venom, the next aircraft
waiting to launch after us, had ditched, following a Flame-
Out on its launch from the catapult.

I called "Carrier-Control' for permission to remain
circuiting until the 'Downed' Venom crew were rescued,
but after two circuits we were directed to continue our usual
vectored sortie. The Boss R/T'd me to remain on our 'C'
Flight R/T Channel, in case we needed to be diverted to a
land-base should it become impossible to recover on-board,
and I was wondering where that might be? I was trying
not to think about the ditched aircraft and the crew, who

would have frozen to death almost instantly, and recalled one of the thoughts I had whilst on the Cat waiting for my launch, that even if I had been hit by squalling waves there would be more than a fair chance of a Skyraider shaking it off, and gaining height, but not a jet, which would suffer an immediate 'flame-out'.

We completed our sortie after nearly two hours flight-time and prepared for Recovery, even though the ship was 'dancing' all over the place, and visibility down to almost zero. I let the Boss go first because I suspected that he might 'Bolt' on his first approach, and in fact he 'Bolted' twice; which unnerved me but I kept my distance until 'Control' cleared me for recovery, despite the weather and heavy sea-spray, I opened the cockpit canopy as a precaution in case of ditching, and warned the other two in the rear cockpit to be ready for a possible 'Ditch'.

I picked up on the Glideslope and could just about make-out the blurred lights on the Landing Mirror through the heavy sea-mist, and kept correcting for sudden gusts of cross-winds and up-draughts; but with so much movement of the Deck in these circumstances I was forced back to a more primitive combination of flying by instinct, by 'Feel' and 'Talk-Down', (otherwise known as flying by the seat of your pants) and just as I got the 'cut' signal, the ship dropped about fifty feet, and the 'meat-ball' flew off the top of the mirror, and my line of sight just below the top of the ship's Island, a red-flare spun-up from behind the Mirror, and Johnny Eagle shouted 'Power! Power!' but I had already slammed the throttle fully home and felt my 'Girl' twist into a left roll, quickly corrected with sharp right-rudder, and up and away and back onto my recovery pattern, picking-up the lights on the mirror; I was back onto the Glide-scope. The ship was still heaving, but my eyes had adjusted more to the glare around the Island, and I knew that if I held my descent, I would pick-up a middle wire. Johnny repeating 'Steady! Steady!' my only worry that the ship would suddenly heave-up as I touched-down; I cut when signaled. I was down, but it was still a dodgy and clumsy landing, one of my worst in fact, a 'brutally' heavier touch-down than I'd hoped for, catching the last (fourth) wire, my main wheels skidding and slipping on the wet saturated deck, unsure about applying brakes, as I was un-hooked from the Wire.

I could hardly see anything as I taxied forward, to park on the starboard quarter (Fly-One); I couldn't see how close I was to the edge of the Deck. The atmosphere on the Flight Deck was tangibly gloomy as I was helped out of the cockpit; the Boss and I were the only two to be launched that day, besides the ditched Venom, and after our recovery the ship changed direction, probably to ride-out the heavy gales that were whipping up the surface-waves that would be capable of causing 'flame-outs' of launching jets. We struggled towards the ship's Island in our soaking heavy Goon-suits, with their sown-in rubber boots, and climbed down one set of stairs to the 'Ops Room', and were instructed to write reports on the weather 'conditions' during our launch. Someone who had watched our recovery casually asked me if I had been scared; I didn't need to think about my reply; "Not scared", I replied, "but swamped by the chilling demand to concentrate so intensely, all my attention focused on catching a wire!"

I guessed there would be an investigation later, but already I had visualized the circumstances, and quite possibly that the Catapult might have either malfunctioned or had been operated too late, when the bow of the ship had been moving on the 'down' rather the 'on the rise,' in which case the Venom would have been thrust downwards into the heavy sea-spray, which would have caused an immediate flame-out and a rapid ditching. The only possible chance of surviving in these circumstances would be by ejecting as soon as possible as the ditched aircraft sank! But I knew then that these first thoughts, as I wrote my report could not be included, but would stay in my memory and continue to haunt me for some time to come. (in fact still do!)

Some of the Air Traffic Controllers seemed to avert their gaze as I went down to the 'Aircrew Ready-Room', or was I being over-sensitive? There was definitely a solemn atmosphere throughout the ship and in the afternoon a Memorial Service was held in one of the Hangars, but what I picked-up on most of all were the doubts about the possible causes and the pointlessness of attempting to fly in such conditions, when there was no real need. I also had the uncomfortable feeling that the Observer in the ditched Venom, had been my distant friend; the 'Ginger' boy from my old school; but I couldn't be sure! Of course I attended the Memorial Service and kept thinking about this! I think we all felt a moral obligation to attend; a shatteringly somber affair, perhaps all of us thinking along similar lines, thinking at moments like this, our thoughts moving towards obvious and simple questions such as: why not me, and if next time, might it be me?

The heavy seas and blustery gales continued for a further three days despite the ship holding to a course intended to take us out of the storm, so further flying was on hold and we busied ourselves with other tasks around the ship until weather conditions changed, but by then we were within reach of plenty of land-based military air-strips. So flying resumed, flying our usual AEW sorties, between the islands of the Northern Orkneys and the Outer Hebrides, and over the famous Fair - Isles and down the East coast as far as the Firth of Forth with its famous bridge. It was in these relatively settled waters that Albion steamed up and down, awaiting the rest of the fleet and the two other Carriers; Bulwark and Eagle in preparation for the Royal Review, which seemed a long time coming so there was still time for some mini-exercises and further ship-painting.

And eventually something like early Spring weather lightened the mood, and other ships of the Fleet started assembling along the coast at the entrance of the Firth of Forth, awaiting the Royal Yacht, HMS Britannia escorted by a Cruiser and several Frigates, which were to lead the Fleet into the Forth into perhaps the last grand display of our rapidly shrinking numbers. But despite our depletion we could still muster an impressive strike force, as we had proven recently at Suez, but perhaps this really was to be the final-salute to the Sovereign of the one-time world's strongest navy.

Britannia and the Cruiser led the two parallel lines of Frigates, followed by Albion, Bulwark and Eagle with enough Royal Marine bandsmen on-board the Carriers to fill the air with martial music; the Royal Fleet Review had begun. The ships anchored in an arc and lit-up at night were like toys on display, and Her Royal Highness, Queen Elizabeth and The Duke of Edinburgh reviewed the Fleet from the Royal Motor Launch and were cheered as they passed each ship, and the Royal Couple finished by spending an evening with us on-board Albion; Dining in the Wardroom and to be Entertained by the ship's Company' in the decorated Hangar which had been draped with bunting and large flags; I think I even managed to just about wriggle into one of the Official photographs taken on that occasion, which of course is another story!

And then after a few runs ashore in Edinburgh after the show was over it was Home Again, at last, perhaps?

Of course before the ship entered Portsmouth all the squadrons flew off and returned to their bases; 849 'C' Flight to Culdrose, and the others to Yeovilton I think, and after a week we were all on a relatively long leave, with all the money jingling in our pockets we had been unable to spend for nearly half a year, and now to pick-up from where I left off last September, nearly eight months before. But of course any tentative relationships with any girls had long-since evaporated - long ago.

I was invited to a few parties and had what I suppose should be seen as a few innocent one-night 'Flings', but nothing serious, and the strangeness of 'lodging' back at home with my mother for company seemed like a backward step which left me with feelings of isolation. Some of my ex-school pals I met were already preparing for marriage or seriously courting while my main attachment was to the RN, or my Squadron, and it might have been this condition that female company picked-up on. Not that I was in any hurry to 'settle-down', but it seemed that somehow I ought to start taking 'life' in that direction a little more seriously; and a girl-friend seemed like a step in that direction. There were places I wanted to visit and the company of the 'right' female companion would have added to certain shared-experiences which are not possible alone.

Maybe I was too inexperienced to attract the right kind of girl; not that I knew what the right kind of girl might be for me! And so my four- week's leave fizzled-out and I returned to my squadron at Culdrose, not with a new girl-friend but with my new bright-red TF model MG sports car.

CULDROSE REVISITED

It was early Summer and Cornwall is a Summer-Holiday place, and 'Basher' (John) Sullivan and I would sometimes drive into Helston for a few quiet pints and a stroll around town, and during one afternoon we were picked-up by a couple of local girls who had obviously sized- us- up as being from the Air Station, and we ended-up going for drinks and enjoyed the obvious tame flirting and the amusing local gossip, and even got as far as discussing future dates. But after John and I discussed our preferences, again it worked out that the one I preferred, John also preferred, so that is how we finished up, and although there was plenty of flirting, our arrangements seemed more like a mutually friendly foursome than personal romances, but was still lots of fun. And for the two months or so, that the Squadron remained at Culdrose, flying the usual sorties, and maintaining our Operational Readiness.

Paddy Niblock, who had managed to get his feet under the table of his (new) girl-friend had managed to immerse himself in the local culture of Helston, and had agreed to dance the Furry Dance, which apparently required a lot of practice, and for which he somehow managed to get 'special leave'. I think he was in the town almost every day, so for a few weeks he was excused flying duties (by permission of the Air Station Captain)

Of course we all attended the occasion of the dance, which had originated so long ago that no one could determine when it began, but it was obviously an ancient fertility ritual, and attended by everyone in the town. Paddy and his partner together were one of a hundred or more 'pairs', the men in white trousers and the ladies in white skirts, each wearing a sprig of 'Lilly of the Valley' flowers, symbols of (their?) virginity (or so I was informed), men wore the flowers, pointing up, on their left breast, the ladies on their right breast, pointing down, and as Helston town's main street runs down a very steep hill and the route of the dancers, starting at the top of the town, have to dance in and out of the houses, to the bottom, and then cross over to the other side of the road, and dance themselves up to the top again, to the accompaniment of a traditional tune, 'The Floral Dance', played by the town's Brass Band; repeated over and over again' ad-infinitum! Paddy danced amazingly well, and with surprising seriousness, and despite some of his squadron mates (me included) trying to distract him, he maintained his composure, and danced his girl off her feet; actually we all commented how good they looked together! And afterwards, most of the squadron retired to the 'Blue Anchor', an equally ancient provider of home-brewed beer, which 849 Squadron-C Flight officially adopted as our watering hole. Apparently they claimed to have been brewing beer, out the back of the Pub, for more than six centuries!

John and I, with our vaguely-attached girls, who were less ambitious than Paddy Niblock, visited surrounding local beauty spots and beaches and went to the Town's tiny cinema occasionally, and many other visits to the Blue Anchor, and then towards the end of Summer had to leave the Girls and return to our ship, which was returning to the Med via Lisbon, where we were expecting to stay for more than a week.

LISBON

The part of Lisbon near the sea was a typical 'sailors' run ashore, with restaurants and 'entertainment' Bars and Girls, and I thought I was safely attached to a group of fellow junior-officers, all of us in Civvies, but somehow I found myself suddenly alone. Now I'm not quite sure how this happened or how I met Alicia, who was a small-boned, petite, alluring local Lisbon lady with beautiful wide-awake eyes and a husky voice. But it didn't take long for me to discover that one of her favourite ways of passing time was to share a leisurely meal in an expensive restaurant with a view of the sea, which as it happened was how we spent the afternoon. Sitting at a small square table facing a window, with a view of the sea, she seemed decent company, but throughout the whole meal, from time to time she leaned over her plate towards me, staring into my face and feeding me snippets of food from her plate, and puckering her lips seemingly throwing kisses as she ate, and keeping me entertained with her funny stories about her friends and her other encounters; I was slightly tipsy and overwhelmed by her attention, and I suppose fascinated by what appeared to be her 'seduction technique'; which only slightly bothered me, on account that our apparent intimacy might appear to other diners as that of a Hostess and her new Sailors-Boyfriend! And

I had been wondering how I might extricate myself from this brief encounter without too much embarrassment! My pathetic excuse was that I must report for duty before eight, and sighed with relief as she waved me farewell from the Quayside as I climbed into the ship's Cutter.

As soon as I was safely back on-board I immediately began imagining all sorts of dangerous possibilities had I stayed longer, and already contemplating whether I should continue to keep my (vague) promises to see her again before we sailed. She was stunningly attractive and enchanting, but thankfully 'common-sense' prevailed. Strangely something similar had happened to some of the others who had gone ashore with me; which they put down to an occupational hazard; I called it a close-shave!

And so back to the Med, exercising around the coast of Malta and being able to fly again over Suez to observe the clearing operation of submerged ships intended to sabotage our operations. The Navy House was still a burned-out ruin, which no doubt stood as a reminder to the Egyptians of our so-called Suez Affair. So after a few more months of our ship loitering between ports in the Med, we were back into the Atlantic on a mini- NATO-exercise, my last on 849 as it happened, as I had completed my time on a Front-Line squadron; to be replaced by others who would maintain the sqadron's readiness. It was from the Mid-Atlantic that I flew my last Skyraider sortie from Albion, returning to Culdrose, and then onto my new posting at Boscombe Down.

EXPERIENCE AND MEMORY

Perhaps it is only as we grow older that we come to reflect on our past experiences, which we think of simply as memories, as if real-lived events can ever be that; one-dimensional images like photographs, to be stored in our heads; but that is what people seem to think. For although we might be unable to grasp much of the meaning at the time of such events, probably because there is too much happening for us to figure it out and absorb things, these experiences eventually come to change us and shape us. Becoming part of us, making us who we are! I suppose that is why I am now able to step-back in time and 're-live' these events of more than half a century ago, as if somehow I am still there in the thick of it, complete with smells and sound effects.

As an event, the so-called Suez Affair was nothing to brag about, in fact my life has changed so much and so many times since then, that I rarely have cause or reason to reflect on it; it is only occasionally that I find myself drawn back to those events, when, perhaps a small reference to it pops-up on a News programme, and then only when some uninformed news-reader presents an impossibly incorrect 'picture'; and one I cannot recognize, as someone who was once there! Then it is at these rare moments that surprise myself, hardly believing that I had been part of any of this!

But 'Suez' is frequently referred to as the turning point in Britain's status as a world power; and Suez was almost the last occasion when Albion, both the Country and Ship of that name, would assert their 'rights' in any time-honoured 'traditional' way. But if Nelson's ghost had been able to pass through Her Majesty's Ship Albion, the Albion I knew, there would still be much there he would be able to recognise from his own times. And not only in the physical differences of the living quarters of Officers and Men, forward and aft; for these differences still enshrined the 'essential' distinctions which still ran through the whole navy, from top to bottom, between officers and men; who in effect inhabited two separate and different worlds. And it was that 'social' friction (fiction?) between these two worlds, as much as any technological and political changes, which gave way to the start of the modernization of our Navy, which I witnessed.

When I read current advertisements for today's navy, it is barely recognizable; everyone seems so civilized and nice (and perhaps too 'tame') in this Brave New (Navy) World. The essential difference, besides appearances and uniforms is that today recruitment is all about GCSEs, 'A' levels, and Trades, whereas in my day it was about adventure; regretfully Jack me-hearty has been replaced by a pseudo-modern Jack me-ringbolt! (modern would-be sailors will not put that in their pipes to smoke it; their ships are probably covered in No Smoking signs!

Alas, Jolly Jack Tar is no more, but now looks and dresses more like a member of a large bland business corporation.

Sadly in my time, the RN, 'The Andrew', 'The Puss' of the 1950's was already on the cusp of that dire change, and enjoying the last halcyon days when 'Up-Spirits' was still piped at 11:30, and 'Hands- Off cocks, and On-Socks' was still piped at 06:00 Reveille, etc.etc. when some of those aspects of Royal Navy life and tradition were still generally appreciated by sailors as some kind of compensation for their 'rougher' and 'tougher' living conditions. But for those in the Fleet Air Arm, whilst these distinctions still held to some extent, there was another necessary factor operating; sometimes contradictory to proper 'Naval Discipline'-principles, and that was the necessary relationship between aircrew and ground-crews (so-called); aided and abetted by new technologies. (a kind of democratization!)

Aircrew (mostly officers) depended for their safety on the skills and knowledge of technicians and engineering ratings; aircraft engine and airframe mechanics, electricians, radar technicians, armourers, parachute- packers, meteorologists, and photographers; and the Skyraider, which had been one of the most advanced propeller-powered aircraft of it's times had enjoyed its reputation for dependability mainly because of its strict servicing regime. Skyraiders of 849 Squadron, had Daily, Weekly and Monthly, as well as Pre-Flight inspections, and when not flying, were in the hangar where further checks or minor repairs were made; these aircraft were maintained to the highest levels, and because of this aircrew were able to do their job with confidence. During my time with 849 Squadron I cannot recall a single incident resulting from inadequate aircraft maintenance!

And besides the highly skilled men who maintained the aircraft, there were also Adimistrators, Supply-Branch ratings, Cooks and Stewards, and even two Regulators (RN military) Police; all who were essential for the self-sufficiency of the Squadron. In fact each aircraft had its own dedicated maintenance crew, and our supply branch, and pay branch ratings, cooks and stewards, whilst belonging to the squadron; during the time the squadron was on-board, became part of that ship's operating departments, and only shifted when the whole squadron moved from one place to another. When the squadron temporarily left the ship to go to Hal Far in Malta, for example, we took everyone of the squadron with us, and while we depended on them, and knew them personally, we were still expected to follow traditional Royal Naval protocols between officers and men!

Among its complement, Albion also had several cats, which kept well-clear of the Ward Room, but attached themselves to particular mess-decks, and in a sense became members of that mess. They would sleep during the day and were usually on duty at night, hunting cockroaches and rats, and usually displayed their kills in the morning. Nobody knew where they came from, but sailors considered themselves very fortuate if their Mess had the good luck to be adopted by a cat. Perhaps in some sense a ship's cat embodied something of the feminine, choosing to curl up on a particular bunk, and then on a whim, settling down for a while with somebody else.

BOSCOMBE DOWN

There is no knowing what mysterious forces are at work, or how or why Service personnel are posted hither and dither, perhaps on some off-chance, from one place to another; which perhaps like life itself is a lottery! And in my case that lottery took me from an enchanted world of the loveable-lumbering Guppy-Skyraider aboard Albion and Culdrose, to almost the completely opposite; to the cutting-edge testing demands of the very latest Naval aircraft; Scimitar, Sea Vixen and Buccaneer. But my route there was via a brief diversion; an introductory and very brief aeronautical engineering course in Arbroath, Scotland (another Royal Naval Air Station) and a Jet's -Conversion course, and then onto A&AEE Boscombe Down; an almost hidden airfield at the top of a hill on a country-road rising out from the small village of Amesbury, Wiltshire; whose sudden main attraction became the dark-haired girl- 'AB' (I have to be careful!), who could quite easily have been the long-lost unknown sister of Jean, the girl of my first innocent encounter with a girl, way back in the 1950's.

My arrival at Boscombe Down and my first impressions were that my posting here was going to be some kind of exile; when the narrow country road, up-hill from the sleepy village of Amesbury, came to a sudden impass at the entrance of A&AEE Boscome Down, where a small cluster of military-looking buildings somehow screened-off the aircraft hangars and runways, which were further protected by a high barbed-wire fence and a guard-house with a security gate, manned by MOD Police; who had anticipated my arrival. They already knew who I was and even registration number of my car.

It wasn't exactly a welcome, more a brief interrogation, after which I was shown to my accommodation to unload my things and taken onto the Officers Mess, which was more RAF than RN; not that this bothered me, because the atmosphere inside was more like a country pub than either; and that is where I was eventually welcomed by the rest of the Naval aircrew, and discovered that I had been specially recommended for that posting; some kind of complement I suppose!

After lunch I was taken to 'C Flight's' hangar, the very small Royal Navy's base along the hard-standing. Just one small hangar, housing five aircraft and two crew-rooms! When I arrived there were two Scimitars and a Sea Vixen, for various trials, but surprisingly, tucked-away in one corner was a beautiful yellow Tiger Moth, which I was immediately drawn to, and in another corner, the strangest aircraft anyone could have imagined! A shiny stubby insect-like creature with a bulbous helicopter-style cockpit, with small delta-wings and long-spindly under-carriage legs, all contributing to it's bumble-bee-like appearance; but even more eccentric, as if it's designers had been making a point, it's lack of paint; it's surfaces highly polished; making it the most strange and exotic flying machine, which I was soon to learn was a prototype VTOL (vertical take-off and landing) vehicle, from Short-Brothers in Ireland, the SC1. And perhaps to further add to it's uniqueness, this strange creature was left in the care of an equally diminutive Irish-man, who wasn't an engineer, but a retired Irish champion boxer, an obvious pugilist by his injured features, whose sole duty was to spend each and every day polishing it's aluminium frame with metal-polish (wadpole). I was to spend many hours listening to his stories of his many fights and many lives.

Although 'C Flight' was a very small unit, it's range of work was wide-ranging and truly experimental, and I quickly came to realize that the other pilots were all, in one way or another, unusual; not quite eccentric, but each with a particularly individual approach to test-flying. There was even one Polish, ex-RAF pilot who had managed to fly a Scimitar backwards, very briefly; by pulling out of a shallow-dive and quickly throttling back to create a controlled-stall, and in-effect sliding back in a shallow-arc. So I wasn't sure where I would fit-in? But I needn't have worried myself about this; for their work-ethic was governed by an almost school-boyish enthusiasm to plan and conduct trials and tests in sometimes creative but always analytical ways. Testing an aircraft's 'flying and operating performance' is mainly about trying to imagine a pilot's 'extreme' demands and expectations of an aircraft, and it's operational requirements, and then 'reproducing' these in real-time. My own introduction to this way of thinking was in contributing to testing the effects of firing the four 30mm cannon on a Scimitar's mainframe (which I still cannot comment on after all these years) All I can say is; that firing cannon of this size whilst flying at high- speeds is not as easy as one might imagine, and the effects on the aircraft;

especially it's outer-skin can be hazardous, but the fun of it can also be exhilarating, and perhaps the closest thing one can experience to playing a modern Video-Game!

The Tiger-Moth, I discovered was used mainly for observing and photographing 'take-offs' and 'landings' of Jets, at least that was the 'Official' reason for having it, and was great fun to fly; "C" Flight pilots even shared her at week-ends, for 'Jollys' around the airfield. But the little 'Short SC1' was purely experimental, and on a strict manufacturer's basic testing schedule, which at this stage had only one engine installed. It was very light and only capable of conventional forward flight, but alas, I never actually saw it fly.

All flying trials were intense and required weekend flying, which meant sometimes over-flying cross-the-channel countries, with occasional Sunday afternoons, nipping down to Switzerland and back before tea. But much of the Testing became routine, sometimes repeating flights many times and amassing data, not unlike working in a laboratory. And as trials-schedules progressed, I also progressed onto short sea-trials, with deck-landings, etc.(a few weeks at a time). But there was also plenty of fun, with entertainments and Dances in the Officer's Mess, and of course my first real love affair with AB., the dark-eyed girl from Amesbury. AB was not at all interested in aircraft, but loved the thrill of 'flying' in the Erica Jong sense of the term; with enough 'flights' to fill a 'log-book', had we bothered to record them, and she also loved my bright red MG.

Most of our courting was conducted in the evenings, with country-walks in and around Amesbury, and after a while we would be invited to accompany her parents on their weekend 'afternoon drives' in her fathers magnificent black and chrome Ford V8 Pilot, highly polished Al Capone-style car; (I think they regarded as a treat for us) cuddling on the back-seat, with the heater blasting away and listening to the radio while her parents chatted in the front seats, as if we weren't there, snuggling-up together wrapped in a thick tartan-car-rug; this was unimaginable 'togetherness', and with great promise; in fact I even got as far as the 'engagement ring', but things fell apart as the Carrier Trials demanded more of my time, and shortly after I received a sudden posting to a Scimitar squadron at Yeovilton; which led to a change of place and change of girl. Perhaps I was becoming a proper Sailor after all!

Actually AB deserves a whole volume to herself; but this is supposed to be about flying in the conventional sense, and how my eternal love affair with the Spad changed my life!

YEOVILTON

By the time Scimitars became operational, they had already acquired 'an unlucky' reputation. The aircraft was big and heavy and not really suited for small-sized Centaur-class carriers; in many ways it was an aircraft out of its time, and naval flying was already changing; perhaps Suez really had been our last proper 'fixed-wing' operation! From now on, helicopters were taking-over to become airborne troops-carriers, and RN pilots more like taxi-drivers. There were still Skyraiders flying from Yeovilton, and occasionally I would find myself following one along the perimeter while I was making ready for take-off, in my now 'screaming' Scimitar, and my heart would miss a beat as I watched it take to the air; but there were also the new turbo-props AEW Gannets, with their Guppy-like raydomes, coming along, waiting to replace the Guppy Spad, and other activities to replace my flying; Wrens for a start!

On Royal Naval Air Stations it is impossible to ignore them, although at Culdrose there had been too few to worry anyone, but there was one in particular I remember, called Charlie, a muscular Amazonian, who surprised me one early morning, when I was Officer of the Day attending the raising of the Flag, by playing Reveille better that any

Marine Bugler, and after I had complimented her for that, she then demanding to know why she was denied Grog. The only reason that came to mind was that, although she was an excellent Bugler, she wouldn't be able to grow a beard, to which she claimed that had not been permitted to 'stop-shaving'. Apparently she was quite capable of growing a full-set!

At Yeovilton Wrens were everywhere, and were also part of that 'Great Change' which was beginning to permeate the RN, and which, among other things, stopped the sailor's daily 'Tot', exchanged Hammocks for fold-away bunks and other bits of 'pampering' including the ending of Blue-liners (three hundred free cigarettes each month),etc.ect., and so it was impossible, not to occasionally find one's self dallying and flirting, and perhaps even being fitted-up for a date with a Wren.

My first encounter was with a very pretty air-mechanic Wren, who won me over me by telling me about her 'fantasy' ideal man; which I soon realised was nothing like me, but based on the hero of a book she had been reading, and who, appropriately was also a Naval Officer by the name of James Bond. I had never heard of him up to this point, but she showed me the book, which she carried everywhere, in her Wren's shoulder-bag, and eventually even coaxed me into reading it; promising me that if I read it, she would consider a date with me. It sounded like blackmail, but she had an irresistably naughty twinkle in her eye, and I took the book as a guide to what I might expect; I wasn't disappointed! And as our relationship deepened we began to enjoy a mutual kind of companionship which absorbed all my energies and interests, and which perhaps was too good to last. (This also deserves a book on its own!)

At the pinnacle of our passions she left the WRNS, and I 'shifted' to Northern Ireland, on 'Security Duties', in other words a 'rest' from flying duties, with resonances, coincidentally, of a 007 life-style, (the hero I had been asked to emulate) but in my case without the Biretta, and chasing wild Irishmen along the desolate Northern/Southern Irish border.

To prepare me for my Security Duties I had to undergo a six weeks (I think) what was then termed a 'Wooly-Head Course', run by a team of mad Royal Marines Commandoes; which was a kind of very short course on handling small-arms, interrogation methods, and working undercover. (Was I now, at last also learning how to kill?) Whilst on the course we had to run everywhere, and I became very fit, and for a while become a sort of soldier, out on very different kinds of sorties. Usually driving in Land Rovers, between Belfast and a Military Radio- Communications Compound at Limavady, and patrolling along the Irish Border between Derry and Donegal, in the bleakest winter days and nights, along mud-track roads, expecting to be ambushed at every turn!

During odd week-ends we practiced 'attacks' on the deserted ex-Naval Air Station Eglinton, with its over-grown runways, which we sometimes used for car-racing; and on one occasion over-turning a hired car, several times! And sometimes out on patrols looking for 'reported suspects' in tiny villages along the Border. There were always 'incidents' to engage, and for a while it was very much more a game of soldiers.

And then after my stint of six months running around the Irish country- side, I was moved onto a Desk job at Arbroath, Scotland, where I (sort of) fell in love with another Wren, petite and lively, who loved singing; especially songs from Rogers and Hammerstein's musicals. (and always; "I'm Gonna wash that Man right-outa my hair!")

ARBROATH

By that time I had become quite a good fencer (Foil and Sabre) and had already attended an advanced 'Fencing Course' at the Royal Marine Barracks, Chatham, and taught my singing-Wren to Fence, and later she also became a crack-shot at Bisley, but eventually married someone from the RAF; much to my regret; but I could console myself that this was also, necessarily part and parcel of learning about my romantic failures and the allure of women, and the dangers of 'love'; and also of the strange intervention of eternal recurrences, (or so it seemed).

In recalling this interlude, another distant memory emerged from that time; an almost completely forgotten incident whilst at Chatham, on the Fencing Course, (provided by the Physical Instructors School there, because the Iner-Services Champion Fencer was a Royal Marine), which included short-courses for all ranks, officers and other ratings; but we all wore the same dark-blue track-suits, without headgear, and were encouraged to run (not walk) between the Gym and living quarters.

On one occasion, I was stopped by a young and over-enthusiastic Royal Marine carrying a big stick under his arm (which meant nothing to me) and he shouted at me so loudly and with such fury that I felt stunned by it. I could see immediately that he was angry and assumed that I had transgressed in some way, by running on the grass or something. He asked me why I hadn't saluted him, and I tried to explain that I was unaware that I was required to, and politely informed him that I was also an Officer and on a Fencing Course, and not required to wear head-gear whilst wearing a track-suit. He seemed ruffled and didn't like this, and spluttered something about what it meant to be a Royal Marine Officer, and I told him that it seemed to me that almost all Royal Marines, of whatever rank and standing carried sticks. He went uncontrollably berserk at this! Spluttering, … "Marines carry small sticks, and Officers carry big sticks, …Sergeants …little sticks, …Officers, …Big Sticks….Get It!" I instantly sensed that he must have had some psychological problem, and ran off.

But among the other odd things which happened whilst at Arbroath; was a strange adventure which began one dark evening when I trekked across country and got lost, and had been circling round the same woods, passing the same farm, until eventually a voice from a clump of trees asked me if I was lost. I couldn't see anyone but continued my conversation with the voice, a dour Scottish voice, which eventually invited me into his farm-house for a cup of tea.

He was elderly and had the wirery-frame of someone who was still working, and wore a fixed-stern expression; but despite this he radiated a kind of other-worldly magnetism; we chatted as it got darker; he amusingly fascinated by how a young Sassenach should suddenly alight on his patch.

We had already discussed my reasons for wandering the countryside, and as it got darker still, he kindly offered to drive me back to the Air Station, dropping me at the main-gate. As he wished me goodnight, he told me to call-in anytime; an open invitation I could not resist, and which led to many new and long-lasting experiences.

The inside rooms of his stone-built cottage were all roughly white-washed, with no decoration or pictures on the walls; even the doors were left unpainted, which as I was later to discover, summed up his whole life-style and his values. He owned two small farms, the other adjacent and farmed by his son; both growing cereal crops and with small dairy-herds, but his main interest was breeding and training horses. I thought I could ride reasonably well, but he taught me how to ride properly, and he also taught me to shoot all sorts of game, and how to prepare what I shot for the pot.

He was over eighty, but still upright and strong, and able to wield a sledgehammer when repairing fences, and bit-by-bit he unraveled, his life-story to me

As the son of a Game-Keeper he had volunteered for the army at the start of the Great War, (First World War) when he was barely sixteen; and before he was seventeen he was in France, and transferred to another Platoon when he and another young Private had been the only survivors of an attack; he managing to survive several other engagements; because as he explained to investigating senior officers at the time, growing up as a Game-Keeper's son, he knew and understood the importance of 'cover'; and how to move across fields without being noticed by Game, or an enemy.

Before his eighteenth birthday he had been Commissioned in the Field, as a Subaltern, and eventually sent to Sandhurst to learn how to use a knife and fork, and later had also been sent to Dublin during the Easter Uprising, where on one occasion he, and his small troop, surrounded by Irish rebels; when he disconnected his armoured vehicle's exhaust-pipe from the silencer, to give the impression of machine-gun fire, and so drove through a barricade; an act of bravery for which he was decorated. Eventually after the war he retired from the army with a 'large purse of money', which enabled him to purchase a small chicken farm, and eventually to own and breed race-horses.

His farm wasn't far from the Air Station, but for me it was like escaping into another world. He also had a (gay) daughter, who owned a dog, but no animals or music were permitted inside the house, and every meal, (even afternoon tea) began with 'Grace', and I soon learned to respect his 'values', and stayed clear of discussing anything that might conflict with them; and so I learned to be more than just a 'Cab Jocky', and eventually, many years later, I came to realise that it was much more than just his 'riding and shooting' lessons that had rubbed-off onto me, through the many weekends I spent being with him. In many ways he was the old-fashion exemplary hero who had truly lived through much more than I could imagine possible, but he took even the most extreme situations quietly in his stride, as part of 'a life'; and in his later years he was still able to maintain those values, and his independence.

And of the singing Wren, who really had hidden depths, a typical English Rose, I might add, and bright and knowledgeable, and who loved Gilbert & Sullivan, and had a nice singing voice! How different might my life had been if I had carried her off to the Altar?

YEOVILTON REVISITED

And then strangely, just as things were becoming interesting once again, a return to RNAS Yeovilton, which became a kind of Grand Finale to my particular 'Game of Sailors'!

I had been applying for all sorts of postings, some which had nothing to do with aircraft or flying; and I assumed that someone at the Admiralty had picked me up on their radar and 'intervened' and directed my posting to a 'non-specific' job of over-seeing several bits and pieces of administration, for example the 'Registering of Replacement aircraft engines', and running several 'Working Parties'; sometimes employing; rum-sodden old-lags and misfits, but best of all, the vital role of "Officer in charge of 'HM's Stables' at RNAS Yeovilton. Yes it might seem odd that a Royal Naval Air Station should have it's own stables, but several very senior officers stationed there, including one admiral, and their wives owned their own horses and frequently rode to hounds at local hunts. And they needed someone in charge of the stables who was sympathetic to that way of life; and as the job included exercising their horses, I was their man!

The job allowed all sorts 'perks'; not least the freedom to run the job as I wished, and to wear what I wanted; but the time of my arrival there was just before the hunting season had begun, and all the horses had been over-fed during winter on oats, and were bloated and needed exercise. Some of the horses hadn't been ridden for months, and were lazy and had become resistant to being ridden, by anyone; hence the job had its dangers. But to ride early-morning through the near-by woods was the earthly equivalence to flying Skyraiders along the Southern-English coast, as the sun came up; a kind of symbiosis with the cosmos at the moment of Creation! (How else can I put it?)

And there were moments of triumph when a 'resistant' horse would finally acknowledge it's rider, and enjoy galloping across a field, and cantering though the trees of the woods when returning to the Stables. And of course the 'appreciation' of their owners, and occasional invitations to 'posh' dinners, for those were the days when horse-ownership was part and parcel of being a very senior officer in Her Majesty's arm forces, and even those of the Royal Navy; certainly as important as their Saville- Row Tailor, their Family, and their Old-School connections. And for me, to run their stable and exercise their Nags, was to be rewarded with 'crumbs from their table' and a kind of freedom from some of the petty-ness of the many silly 'games of sailors'; consequently I was excused all tedious duties and largely left in peace.

I think it was also at Yeovilton that I had the most bizarre experiences whilst in the RN; all crammed into in my final posting; more than all of the others from elsewhere put together! It seemed that someone had lit my blue-paper fuse, and that I had been on a trajectory of experiences, which had taken me to Suez and up to the Artic Circle; from the start as not much more than a fresh-faced boy; but through a series of postings and events, it felt as if I was finally growing up! Some things I had learned the hard way, making my own mistakes, and at other times, from others and their mistakes. With many occasions when things had been going seriously wrong or worse, because of my inadequacy, and when at the last moment something seemed to 'give', to haul me back onboard, to save my skin; I called it luck but it might have been fate, or a guardian angel! There were also times when I knew that I had pushed some boundaries beyond the limits; and the walls had come tumbling - down.

One such daunting 'experience' which started, as I think they all did, in a simple and straightforward and innocent way, began when a newly-promoted Petty Officer came to see me one morning, with what I assumed was a simple request. His story was that he had received a 'sudden' drafting, and that as his wife had only just recently moved to be with him in a small country village, without a telephone, he was desperate to inform her about the sudden (emergency) posting, and that she was to meet him at Yeovil Town railway station, with her things, so that they could travel together to Lossiemouth, in Scotland.

I knew him only as someone who had once been a member of a Naval Fencing team, and who perhaps had been unable to arrange things with another rating. I didn't have the time to consider the usual protocols restricting relationships between Commissioned Officers and other ranks, and as he assured me that there was no one else who was available to help him, and that he was desperately worried about his wife, I agreed to drive to the village, some fair distance, in the heart of nowhere, to inform her.

It was still early morning, and his wife was still in bed when I knocked, but came to the door to learn the news of her husband's sudden posting. She was surprisingly beautiful with long hair, which she was continuously brushing as I tried to give her the instructions. She was obviously shaken by the news, and asked me in, and also if I had the time to drop her off at the station. I couldn't see any way out this, so I agreed.

The cottage was tiny, and as I sat and waited for her to dress and pack her things, she kept moving from one room to another, asking me to repeat her husband's instructions, and prodding for details about how I knew her husband; and when she learned that I was a officer, and not one of his mates, she showered me with apologies and expressions of gratitude. Finally she was ready to go, with very little luggage; and cooed like a little girl when she saw my red MG.

It was a sunny morning and the hood was down, and she tied a head-scarf to cover her hair, as if we were out for a morning ride rather than being ferried to the railway station. She thanked me as she got out, and that was that, or so I thought. Until several days later I discovered that she hadn't been the man's wife, but the wife of another Petty Officer at the Air Station, and that unwittingly I had assisted in their escapade, which had been the reason for the sudden posting. Luckily no one knew of my part in this matter, and I just kept quiet about it. But four or so months later there was a dance in the NAAFI to which I had been invited, and whilst I was watching the dancing couples, a familiar face glanced at me over the shoulder of her dance-partner; and it took me several minutes before I was able to remember where I had seen her before; it was the run-away wife I had taken to the station!

I was surprised and intrigued, and watched her as she circled around the dance-floor, always making eye contact and smiling as she passed by. And after the music had stopped, she moved through the tables and breathlessly asked if I was alone, and then dropped a piece of paper on my table and disappeared back into her crowd. It was one of those moments where common-sense gives way to impulse; her note had a brief message scrawled on a piece of scrap paper, telling me that if I wanted an explanation, to call her, and her telephone number.

Looking back on those times, I know that I should have resisted the compulsions of my curiosity, but each time I read her scrappy note I felt the pull of an adventure, which I knew might be either dangerous or downright stupid. But never-the-less, a few evenings later I found myself dialing her number and being told in a muffled voice that she had been waiting for me to call. She quickly said that she wanted to see me, and asked me to meet her at the end of a road among the Air Station's married quarters. Even as she got into my car I knew I was playing with fire, but she looked dazzling, and I could already understand why someone would wish to abduct her and run away with her. When I asked her where she wanted to go, she simply said, "Anywhere", as if we had both been suddenly disconnected from reality, and re-cast in some make-believe drama, which as events unfolded became increasingly unreal.

We found a small pub a long way from our base, and hid ourselves in a corner, where she attempted to explain events which led up to the time I took her to the station. Her story, as I remember it, was that her lover had left his wife for her mother, (yes her mother!) and they had rented a mobile home near the Air Station, both pretending to be husband and wife, but after a while, he, her mother's boyfriend, met her and they fell in love, which led to them renting the country cottage; but her husband, who was also a petty officer on the Air Station, reported the whole affair to his Divisional Officer, and eventually it all unraveled, which led to the instant posting of her lover, and she returning to her husband and her two young children. (This is a very condensed version of the story)

At this point my head was swimming in a kind of delirium and I felt caught like a fish in a net, not knowing how to, or whether to escape. The way in which she told the story had cast me in the role of her 'hero' who had rescued her, and now she was 'dangling' her charms before me; all I had to do was reach out and she would also be mine! She had edged closer, our bodies touching; she was small, and nothing in her appearance would have suggested anything other than 'pure innocence', or maybe I still hadn't grown up! But I had already bitten the apple!

After several clandestine dates, we ended-up at her friend's house where we had a few drinks, after which she needed to lie down upstairs, which at the time seemed like my good-fortune, but not much later turned out to be contrived and a set-up. Her friend, who was also married, was also on the look-out for a 'boyfriend', and asked me to introduce her to one of my friends, which I did, and which later led to some complicated chain-reactions. But finally everything became so convoluted that it became necessary to escape.

So with one leap, Caruthers was free! And as Rudyard Kipling would say, 'I learned about women from her!'

Another equally bizarre experience also occurred during a dance, a rather more grandiose affair; actually a Fleet Air Arm Centennial Dinner and Dance in the Wardroom, at which the Guest of Honour was the First Sea Lord, with also a scattering of Admirals, and I think also all the King's horses and all the King's men, or nearly all! And it was perhaps this kind of thought, which prompted a young Irish Observer, from one of the squadrons, who vaguely knew me, to visit my stables during the evening, and in the dark saddle a horse and attempt to enter the Ward Room through the open French windows mounted on his charger. This required riding up several stone steps before entering the dinning room, which had been cleared for the evening's entertainments, and into the crowded 'ball-room'. The sudden arrival of a very drunken Irishman on a very large horse, shouting 'Tallyho', created sudden panic and screams among the ladies, frightening the horse, which reared-up and threw its drunken rider. Apparently there was pandemonium, with ambulances and emergency services, and lots of very angry senior officers, with more egg on their faces than on their hats, and the following day me being grilled for 'not making it impossible for 'mad' young officers to night-ride'! He still rides, at night, in my imagination!

There were also many other, too many, lesser bizarre experiences which punctuated my last rare game of sailors, to the point perhaps of ridicule, comparable to a Gilbert and Sullivan operetta; but not everyone saw the funny side of things. Perhaps the gods of mirth sought me out. I once had to accompany a very green young officer on his very first Evening - Rounds, through every Mess on the Air Station, and we finished up at the Guard House, which was only slightly untidy, because the Guard-House cat was still eating from a large dish, but never-the-less it had decided to scatter some of its food on the deck (floor). The young officer, who obviously took life and his duties very seriously, demanded to know what the cat was doing in the Guard House during Rounds, to which the duty Leading-Hand replied, "Eating Dinner Sir! The young Officer of the Day looked at his watch, and then at the food on the floor, and diligently replied, "Dinner finishes at eight thirty, …it's now eight thirty-one!" I wanted to laugh, and so did the Leading-Hand, and I think even the cat looked slightly bemused, but the young officer, seemed not to get it, and looked enquiringly at me straight faced. (I'm not making this up)

NAVAL HUMOUR & LANGUAGE

Humour and language in the Royal Navy has it's own proud (and still unappreciated) history and has been, and still is part of naval 'synergy', enabling it's sailors to 'rule the waves'(after a fashion). Even Nelson, himself, recognised that despite the strict and harsh naval discipline for his sailors, they had a kind of courage which allowed them to laugh in the face of danger and the enemy, (and sometimes naval stupidity) which he boasted as, "Aft the most Honour, For'ard the most Glory", and he knew it was that hard-won 'Glory' which endeared the Jolly Jack Tar to the whole grateful English nation, for their protection from invasion by the French and others, and which we still sing about when we sing 'Rule Britannia'. Of course naval humour and language were both coarse and bawdy, and mostly incomprehensible to 'land-lubbers', because with it's wry cryptic resonances, it allows Jolly Jack to convey information about his 'shared situation' in a flash, to his ship-mates. It's cutting irony, ranging from it's mundane silliness to it's extreme bizarreness; and from the 'almost obvious' to the wickedly existentially cruel, combining truly philosophical wit, as well as 'existential wisdom'; and at it's most gorgeously wicked when puncturing naval and bureaucratic pomposity. Here I'm referring to lower-deck humour, the Real Stuff of the truly 'Ironic', which by comparison, Ward Room humour was Boy-Scout-ishly flaccid!

A persistent memory of this difference, which frequently revisits me, still, was the occasion one dark night (23:00 hrs) on the Flight Deck of Albion, when the ship had run into a force nine howling gale, and the Flight Deck awash with sea spray; and the duty squadron officer mustering the duty 'maintenance' crew, (who would have preferred to have stayed below in the warmth of their Mess) onto the Flight Deck.

The Duty Officer at the time was a 'Hornblower' type, from Dartmouth, who had decided that the Skyraiders on the Flight Deck needed 'double lashings' to hold them down, against the tearing wind. And as each extra lashing was fixed, he checked the tension, advising either 'tighter' or 'another lashing'. At one point, one disconsolate and un-jolly jack exclaimed, from the darkness, "F*** this for a game of Sailors, ...there's enough f***ing lashings to hold down a f***ing Sherman Tank !" It was too dark to see from where the protesting voice had emerged, but Lieutenant Hornblower's voice also rang out like the true Commander and Master he had been trained to be, and immediately replied,

"Maybe a Sherman Tank, ...but not a Sky-raider". (emphasizing the word 'raider' with grim determination) and with such conviction, in his sturdy Parade-ground voice, that the duty crew attached as many lashings to each aircraft as was physically possible in total silence, and after being dismissed and passing down the ladder from the Island, all frozen cold and soaking wet, then exploded into shrieks of wicked laughter!

My experience was, that there was hardly a moment whilst in charge of any working parties, or even preparing for a flight, that their so-called 'lower-deck humour failed to highlight the amusing absurdity of a 'game of sailors'! In fact it was this 'quality' which I associate most with the Andrew of my days, which seems to me to have much diminished since those times. I also recall that Night flying entitled aircrews to a night-flying dinner, (something more than a snack to sustain us), usually mash and a small individual steak & kidney puddings; so full of meat that they burst through their pastry on the plate, which the cook on duty referred to as 'babies-eads', (they looked a bit like that), and on another occasion when walking across the deck to my aircraft I dropped one of my gloves, which was instantly retrieved by an, (un-known to me) aircraft-handler, who scooped it up in one graceful balletic movement and handed it to me, and before I could thank him, he simply said; "Glovely!". That poetically magical use of language, which was so naturally spontaneous, stuck with me long after I left the navy, and carried me through my other vocations. And as for the constant use of the word-'Fuck', which on the lower-deck of my time was not considered offensive language, but used only to give emphasis to a statement! (although rarely used by officers).

But perhaps naval humour, or rather the jokes are only funny when told at Tot-time, which alas is no more, or in the NAAFI. I have heard too many that I no longer remember any, but they were all tinged with that same essence of madness; and too rude to repeat!

Almost certainly, the new employees of the modern navy have things much easier than before, but I doubt they will have as much fun, or as many opportunities to deviate from the straight and narrow, of a now almost evangelical bureaucratic life-style. I don't count my own personal experiences to be all that unusual for those times, and I don't see myself as an old sailor, we worked hard and we played hard, and we came out the other end with more than we signed-up for!

And now in the dreams of my dotage, I imagine myself more like Dylan Thomas's old blind Captain Cat, from Under Milk Wood; drifting, "down salt-deep into the Davy dark where the fish come nipping and nibbling me down to the wishbone"; and the long drowned, especially the crew of that ditched Sea Venom, off the Albion, "muzzling up to me" in the frozen waters of the Artic. And re-visiting, in my mind's eye, the over-grown redundant runways of the several Air Stations scattered around Britain, and remembering some of the crazy antics that young men perform when they are indomitably and youthfully immortal!

INTERLUDE & PRELUDE

And then suddenly no longer immortal, but looking for something to do! And after four academic terms at Brasted Place College, Kent, 'thinking and praying', which was to become my Wordsworthian 'Prelude', I hit the road for a few weeks, like Jack Kerourac, looking for Freedom and Meaning.

I didn't do much more than hitch-hike around England, visiting many places I had seen only previously from the air; and I was now one of those tiny dots I would have glimpsed scurrying along empty country roads somewhere, alone and going nowhere in particular. And almost by a circuitous route back home to Fulwell Road, to ponder what to do to earn some cash.

For a brief few months I worked for BA at Heathrow, logging repairs to aircraft and learning to assess commercial aircraft 'faults', but the atmosphere was too much like a factory, and one afternoon I just quit after being 'instructed' that I was required to work 'shifts'. I reasoned that if I had wanted shifts I would have signed on for a few more years in the Andrew! And then out of the Blue,(and the strength of my time at Boscombe Down) I was offered a job as a

Ken Evans

Test Engineer at BAC Bristol, on a new project developing a supersonic passenger plane, to be named Concorde. Apparently another ex-Tester from Boscombe Down had just joined the project and recommended me.

CONCORDE

Yes, it's true, the RN really does prepare you for Civvy Street, in more ways than one.

My initial work was to design and write flight-tests instructions, concentrating on three functions; hydraulic actuation of the engine Variable Intakes, the Droop-Nose actuation, and Airbrakes. This meant that I worked between Toulouse and Filton in Bristol, and whilst in Toulouse, staying in the best hotel, and eating in the best Restaurants. And as I usually didn't finish work until seven or eight o'clock, it meant that I occupied the whole evening working my way through several courses of the finest French cuisine, and getting to know the best wines, and also some of the classy prostitutes who lounged in the glass-covered frontage to the Restaurant, waiting for their Sugar-Daddies, and secret rendezvous; all of them far too attractive and well-dressed to become mere wives! And so I observed a certain French (bourgeois) life-style, and wrapped myself in its elegance!

The Joint British/French Concorde Project required allocating responsibilities for specific parts of the aircraft between the British Aircraft Corporation and the French Sud Aviation, which also required sharing expertise and skills, etc. and besides myself and a handful of very senior designers and engineers, there were technicians from Filton helping to build the French prototype, whose requirement for a Tea-Break in the morning, amused their French counterparts. And interestingly, the brittle social seperation between Officers and Men of the Navy, still operated in both Filton and Toulouse, which meant for me that whilst in Toulouse, I had two hours for Lunch, and was served at Table, with wine, which used to virtually knock me out for the afternoon, so I used to try to fit everything into the long morning. And because Toulouse was very hot, most of the Senior staff took their Siesta; a habit I eventually embraced.

My role was mainly 'Experimental', and fortunately I was able to draw much from my Testing experience at Boscombe Down; but the twin-ramp Air Intakes, which contolled the shock-wave airflow to the engines were cutting-edge, and also the Droop-Nose had never been seen before, and despite the pre-design experiments and testing of these, further development progressed alongside the actual construction. We were always in the Testing Mode, and my Fleet Air Arm connections paid-off in several other ways. Some of the French Test Engineers had similar backgrounds to my own, some of them had also been at Suez, and some had even flown Skyraiders and shared my affections for the Spad; which more than helped oil the wheels of our entente-cordiale. I also came to admire their engineering skills and approach; whenever we met a design problem we tended to approach it from different directions and with different assumptions; my approach was to refer to similar examples or situations, and theirs was to go-back to basic engineering principles. They frequently came up with a complete design-change as the solution, while I was still trying to iron-out the flaws of the original design; they were also great admirers of simple solutions; the simpler the better! And when occasionally they were unable to suppress their natural inclination to their chauvinism, I would also remind them of Crecy and Agincourt, and of Shakespeare's speech on St. Crispin's Day!

But I remember my times in Toulouse more for my peripheral experiences there, and especially the 1968 Student's Revolt, May 6th, the day that university students of the UNFED (Union Nationale des Etudiants de France) paralysed the whole of France with their national strikes, which also drew support from Teachers and Lecturers, and the Fire Services, and other Workers from factories, including those from Sud-Aviation; so for me there was no work that day.

One of the Filton managers called me and suggested that we drive to the countryside for a picnic, organised by his wife, and while I was waiting to be picked up from the hotel, I was suddenly aware of a huge rumbling sound outside in the street; as if heavy machines were being driven along the pavement. From my balcony I could see the main road; a grand main thoroughfare, fifty or so metres wide, with its two main lanes and four side-lanes, with row upon row of students, arms linked with uniformed Fire-men, and hundreds of their supporters, shuffling along the road, ominously silent; only the rumbling-noise of their feet as they swayed along, like a huge human battering-ram. I was shaken and fascinated by this phalanx of sheer human resistance; nothing at all like anything that might ever occur in this way in England; but there was also something grand about it, irrespective of it's reasons. I stood there on that balcony until they marched past the hotel, and out of sight but not out of hearing!

We drove out of Toulouse to first visit Carcassonne, the castle with it's large sign advising everyone to visit it before they die, so we needed to fulfill our obligation; and so after walking along the battlements, climbing the towers, and tasting the local wine, deep in bowels of the near-freezing Castle Keep, we drove south, searching for somewhere for our picnic.

We found our place of tranquility, and drove off the road and walked a while into a vast field of long grass; a gloriously hot summer's day, and spread out our tartan rug, and ate what amounted to a super buffet; salad, sausage, fresh bread, and chilled white wine; the closest experience to paradise, with a gentle warm breeze carrying the aroma of dried-long grass and wild country-flowers.

We chatted, but not about the project, but about everything else; about the French county-side, and the many types of butterflies, and a strange concrete pyramid-like object not far from our feet, but now more visible because we had flattened the surrounding long grass; and we discussed what it might be! It looked like a marker of some sort, we thought probably marking a connecting-point for an underground electrical supply cable, or something like that. But after we walked together further into the field, we discovered many more of them, scattered around in no obvious pattern, and concluded that they might have simply been disposed and dumped there.

And we returned to our picnic spot, and had coffee from a giant thermos; his wife was a perfect picnic-planner! And as the afternoon cooled, and a breeze was getting up we decided to look for a restaurant, and stopped in the next large village, with a few old shops, and worked our way down the main road. Most of the shops seemed to be selling souvenirs, and as we stared in, as we passed, shopkeepers seemed to stare out at us, with a kind of hostility.

We passed small Cafes but we kept going because we could see at the far end of the village, a large restaurant sign, and we were anticipating something cooked, but once inside we encountered a confusing hostility. My host was struggling to arrange a table, but the manager,whose English was less adequate than my French, kept trying to shoo us out of the door; then something clicked. My host, with his light hair and tanned face and his fair-skinned wife had been mistaken for German tourists, and we gleaned from others in a local café, that this was the normal response to anybody resembling Germans. And also discovered the purpose of the stone pyramids in our picnic field. They were markers, marking the spots where men and boys from the village had been massacred by retreating German soldiers, at the end of their occupation, and the pain of that memory still burned all of that generation. And we unknowingly had trespassed onto Hallowed ground!

We moved onto other villages and small towns, and eventually stopped, just as it was beginning to get dark and stopped at a bijou restaurant, with it's few outside round white-marble topped tables being moved under-cover for the night; we implored the owner/manager/waiter, in his long while apron, for a table inside, almost begging and insisting on our Englishness! And luckily, with great Gallic charm and flair, he threw a clean traditional checkered tablecloth across one of the tables, and apologizing for only the remains of the Day's Menu, served delicious soup, cold meats, beef cassoulet, a variety of cheeses, a choice of wine, and freshly made coffee. All served with aplomb, and the final bill, thirty Francs; and we had great difficulty on insisting that he accept a five Francs 'addition'! With satisfied appetites and full stomachs, our appreciation of the feast and his suave nonchalance and savoir-faire, became the main focus of our conversation on the way back to Toulouse, which had now returned to its calm respectability.

The Concorde project was progressing and systems tests moving towards the first test flight, and I was moving back and forth trying to manage tests on both the French and British prototypes. Filton had its own executive jet aircraft, an HS 125 (a so-called executive jet) which we used for ferrying engineers etc, back and forth; for me sometimes twice a week! Sometimes we hit real fundamental problems on the prototypes, caused by confusion between two different (national) design systems, and my tests usually led to identifying design weaknesses and build problems, particularly on the hydraulic system that had to deal with exceptionally high pressures, especially and unusually on the (back) return-pressures, requiring stronger materials in the manufacture of the components (actuators), while at the same time trying to reduce the weight! An almost impossible contradiction at times, but that was our challenge.

Everyone who worked on the project knew that they were making history. Every single item, every pipe or small bracket, had been designed and drawn and manufactured to exacting measurements and from specified materials, and all joined together to make a fully-integrated flying machine, that would carry passengers safely at twice the speed of sound, from one continent to another; and we were doing it for the very first time in history.

And sometimes there were discrepancies between the design drawings and the actual sub-assembly; for example the pipe-work to the air-intake actuators, which had been built with the supply and return piping reversed, to calamitous consequences! But the Testing schedules were meticulous, teasing-out every possible weakness and correcting and improving every single design item; for this was cutting-edge aircraft engineering, and not far from 'rocket science'! So when we watched Andre Turcat taxi the French Prototype: 001 onto the runway for the first flight on Sunday, 2nd of March, 1969, we all knew that she would fly well, but we kept our fingers crossed anyway.

We could feel the power of the four engines at full-throttle shaking the air, as she lifted off. There is no finer feeling than that moment for any pilot, when his Cab unsticks from terra-firma and the machine is entirely in his hands; he and his aircraft instantly becoming subject to an altogether different set of physical laws; not ordinary laws that hold human-kind to terra-firma, but the laws of flight in their mystical formula. Where thrust overcomes drag and lift overcomes gravity and man and machine becomes (so it seems) lighter than air. And on that day the great white bird made history, and time for me to move-on.

Printed in the United States
By Bookmasters